INTEGRATIVE FAMILY THERAPY

CREATIVE PASTORAL CARE AND COUNSELING

INTEGRATIVE FAMILY THERAPY

DAVID C. OLSEN

FORTRESS PRESS   MINNEAPOLIS

INTEGRATIVE FAMILY THERAPY

Scripture quotations unless otherwise noted are from the New Revised Standard Version Bible, copyright © 1989 by the Division of Christian Education of the National Council of the Churches of Christ in the United States.

Interior design: Publishers' WorkGroup
Cover art: Kari Alberg
Cover design: Spangler Design Team

Library of Congress Cataloging-in-Publication Data

Olsen, David C., 1952–
    Integrative family therapy / David C. Olsen.
        p.   cm. — (Creative pastoral care and counseling series)
    Includes bibliographical references.
    ISBN 0-8006-2638-9 (alk. paper)
    1. Pastoral counseling.   2. Family psychotherapy.   I. Title.
    II. Series.
    BV4012.2.057   1993
    253.5—dc20
                                                            92–44125
                                                            CIP

The paper used in this publication meets the minimum requirements of American National Standard for Information Sciences—Permanence of Paper for Printed Library Materials, ANSI Z329.48-1984.   ∞™

Manufactured in the U.S.A.   AF 1-2638

4   5   6   7   8   9   10   11

CONTENTS

ILLUSTRATIONS

FOREWORD

Early in this century, marriage and family (as well as marriage and family counseling) was a secondary field relegated to agricultural colleges and home economics departments. Within academia it was not given the status normally associated with clinical psychology, psychiatry, or social work—and many times people doing marriage and family therapy were thought to be individuals who could not get accepted into those more esteemed programs. Marriage and family was far from a glamorous field attracting the keen minds of the day. Not so anymore.

The field of marriage and family is no longer a tagalong discipline, but now has its own respected university departments. In my assessment it has become the most creative of the mental health sciences today. Its major contribution has been the development of systems theory and the method of counseling based upon it—certainly one of the most important psychotherapeutic developments in this century.

In *Integrative Family Therapy*, David Olsen ties together the work of various marriage and family theorists. The burgeoning field has grown so much and so quickly that, at times, it is difficult to sort out the best work from the rest. Olsen does that—and more. From the works of a number of schools of marriage and family therapy, he has developed an integrative model. Chapter 1 discusses a number of the key theoretical concepts of systems, marriage, and family therapy. Chapter 2 looks at six schools of family therapy, summarizing the key concepts of each. Chapter 3 introduces an integrative model of family assessment. Chapter 4 suggests a method of counseling couples and families using insights from all of the schools of family therapy discussed. The final chapter presents three cases that are treated by the integrative model presented here.

I think you will find *Integrative Family Therapy* a useful book. Olsen does what he sets out to do—provide a model of pastoral counseling for family problems that draws from the best of family systems theory. I urge you to try his model and use it with families who come to you for help.

HOWARD W. STONE

7

PREFACE

Family systems theory has grown enormously in both popularity and clinical application in the last few years. Clergy and pastoral counselors are discovering the clinical usefulness of systems theory to understand not only organizational dynamics, particularly in parishes, but also the dynamics of couples and families. More and more clergy attend family therapy training conferences and read some family therapy literature.

But as the family therapy field continues to grow in terms of literature, workshops, and research, students of the theory, including both clergy and trainees in marriage and family counseling, have increasing difficulty knowing how to apply the abundance of theory. Some cling to the more charismatic figures in the field, attempting to apply one theory and paradigm to every marriage and family problem they encounter. Others are not able to make informed decisions about which theory and set of techniques to apply to which problems. In addition, knowing how to make a clear assessment informed by theory and then building a treatment plan based on that assessment may seem overwhelming. Scanning the literature often does not help, because much of the literature is written from the vantage point of one theory. Little has been written from an integrative perspective, particularly for clergy and pastoral counseling students.

This book is an attempt to fill that gap in the literature. I intend to provide an integrative model that summarizes some major family therapy theories, and then show how to integrate them in forming a map that one can use for both assessment and treatment planning. I include application to both short-term and long-term cases. Although I have written the book for clergy and beginning students of marriage and family therapy, I hope more experienced clinicians will find it useful to integrate theories.

1

PASTORAL CARING
AND THE MAZE OF
FAMILY THERAPY MODELS

Beginning family therapists, parish clergy, and experienced pastoral counselors find that working with families is rarely easy. Family therapy trainees frequently are overwhelmed when they begin counseling a family. Trainees often report not knowing where to start or how to intervene. Pastoral counselors trained in individual models of psychotherapy find themselves ill-equipped to work with chaotic families. Parish clergy who are involved continuously with families and their problems frequently feel inadequate when counseling them.

That even clergy so immersed in the lives of families find family work difficult can be surprising. Clergy are involved in the developmental transitions of family life from birth until death. Clergy perform all the rituals—baptisms, catechisms, weddings, and funerals—that tend to mark liturgically the transitions of family life. Although these are often times of great joy and celebration, clergy are frequently surprised by how complicated these occasions can be. Three examples illustrate this.

1. Pastor Down is called by Lois, a young mother in his congregation whose baby he is to baptize in two weeks. Lois shakily tells Pastor Down that she is thinking about cancelling the baptism because her parents, who have never approved of her marriage to Don, refuse to come. Lois does not know what to do. She and Don have had an intense argument, and Don has told her that if she does not stand up to her parents once and for all, he may leave her.

2. Anita and Mike have asked Rev. Elizabeth Jordan to perform their wedding. When she meets with the couple to review the last-minute details of the wedding, she is caught by surprise as Anita begins to cry. She asks what Anita is feeling, and Anita responds tearfully, "This was supposed to be the happiest day of my life, but it is becoming a nightmare. I wish I had just eloped and saved the grief." As Rev. Jordan pursues more details, Anita explains that her parents are divorced and her father has remarried. Her mother has just announced that she will not come to the wedding if Anita allows her father to walk her down the aisle. She has accused Anita of being disloyal

11

for even inviting her father to the wedding. Anita and Mike do not know what to do and desperately want help from their pastor.

3. Reverend Frank Martin has just arranged the details of a funeral service for Mark's father. Mark has been active in the parish, but his father had been far less active. After reviewing the details of the service, Mark blurts out, "You know, pastor, my father was a drunk! All my childhood I was terrified of him. I used to pray that he would drink himself to death. Now that he's dead I feel nothing. Why should I even go to the funeral?"

These common experiences plunge the clergy, on regular occasions, into the complexities of the family system. Pastors soon find that simply knowing some individual counseling skills has not equipped them to deal with the complexities of family life that they encounter in their congregations. The rapidly changing face of the family makes the task even more difficult. Clergy find that their congregations are composed of fewer traditional families, and they are asked to provide pastoral care to an increasingly large number of single-parent families and blended (remarried) families. These families further complicate the issues that the clergy face. Church events that mark transitions in life, such as those described in the three examples, can become quite complicated. In addition, today's family is largely cut off from the support of the extended family. Thus families are increasingly isolated and without support. When one combines these realities with the fact that many families now need two incomes and hence two careers, it is no wonder that families are under so much stress, and that clergy can experience much confusion and stress in attempting to minister to parish families.

Clergy can utilize Judeo-Christian notions of a covenantal view of the family and can attempt through sermons to apply theological concepts like reconciliation and grace to the family, but too often find that these words are quickly lost in the maze of all the pressures that the family faces. Clergy then frequently feel inadequate and unprepared to minister effectively to the complexities of family life, and do not know where to turn for assistance.

Clergy are not alone in those feelings of inadequacy. Even experienced counselors can be left overwhelmed by the complexity of family problems and confused by what is happening in a family counseling session. Too often counselors and family therapy trainees deal with the chaos by trying to work only with the individual, or falling back to using the same counseling techniques they employed with individual clients.

CLERGY AND THE
FAMILY THERAPY MOVEMENT

Where can clergy go for assistance? For many the answer has been to turn to the family therapy movement, which seems to offer some much-needed help.

Family therapy has become a rapidly growing movement with its own professional organization (the American Association for Marriage and Family Therapy), its own training programs, its own journals, its own research, as well as increasing respectability. Nonetheless, the movement has some problems that complicate counselors' search for answers.

One major problem is the lack of integration of theory. Part of the rapid growth has occurred through numerous family therapy conferences, which have popularized many forms of family therapy. Beginning students or clergy are frequently exposed to the gurus of the family therapy movement doing a live interview of a family or showing videotapes of their work with a couple or family. These presenters are usually quite charismatic, and their work seems to have a magical quality. Mesmerized by the work they see, beginners often go home eager to imitate it, sometimes with disastrous results. Beginners often fantasize about studying with one of the gurus, or at least with one of their disciples, at one of the many freestanding institutes around the country. The increasing demand for training has resulted in the family therapy movement becoming too technique oriented and not teaching students how to integrate the various theories.

A second problem is that many of those who are called upon to provide family therapy have never been grounded in the basics of family systems theory, even though they may have considerable expertise in doing therapy from another modality, often individual psychotherapy. Many clergy have received some basic training in nondirective type counseling and have learned some basic reflective listening skills. This counseling may work quite well with individual clients, particularly those who are bright, introspective, and verbal, but it does not necessarily work well with couples and families. Indeed, trying just to listen may result in the counselor getting caught up in the escalating interaction with the couple or family and may block effective change. Family therapy is not a set of individual techniques applied to a family; family systems theory is a whole new way of seeing and thinking about the nature of problems.

A third problem is that counselors may be overwhelmed by all that is occurring in a session with a couple or family. If they do not have a solid grounding in family systems theory or a fairly well-constructed paradigm that helps them frame all that is happening in the room, they can be lost in a flood of family interactions. The application of individual techniques to the complexity of a family system can bewilder a counselor.

A final problem is that constructing a paradigm for working with families is itself difficult. The popularity of family therapy and the many available paradigms tempts one simply to accept the tenets of one paradigm and use it with whatever type of family one sees. The most difficult task is that of integration. Integration involves studying the basics of systems theory, understanding the major paradigms of family therapy, blending those paradigms, and then applying that unified model to assessment and treatment planning. Despite the difficulty of this task, one must undertake it if one is to work effectively with families.

Thus clergy increasingly turn to the family therapy movement for help in dealing with parish families and other families that they counsel, but using and integrating that help is not as easy as one might think, as the following case study illustrates.

Ken and Marge Randolf consult Pastor Coleman about problems they are having with their oldest daughter, fifteen-year-old Judy. Judy is suddenly having difficulty in high school, and they have received several warning notices that she may not pass her sophomore year. They are also worried that her friends may be having a bad influence on her. The Randolfs are anxiously wondering what to do.

As Pastor Coleman listens to their story he is aware that he could intervene in a number of ways depending on what theories he chooses to apply. With his training as an individual psychotherapist he might decide to see Judy alone and attempt to help her sort out her conflicts. Having just returned from a family therapy conference, he could apply the orientation modeled by one of the presenters. Or he could choose from a number of major theories of family therapy.

How is he to know which of those theories would be most helpful to the Randolf family? Should he work individually with Judy, or only with the couple and coach them how to handle her? Perhaps he should see the family unit. But who should he include in that session? Should he see only Ken, Marge, and Judy, or should he include the two younger brothers so that he can see the entire family unit? Should he go beyond the nuclear family and also see the grandparents, who live in town, to gain a multigenerational perspective?

After Pastor Coleman decides whom he should invite to the session, he must decide the focus of the session. Perhaps he should simply attempt to negotiate a behavioral contract between Judy and her parents whereby they would reward her if she were more successful in completing her assignments. Or, knowing that many problems are related to communication, perhaps he should try to understand the communication style of the family and help them change the way they communicate, thereby ameliorating Judy's problem. Another possibility is to examine the family structure, looking for inadequate boundaries, triangles, or possibly a troubled marriage, believing that Judy's problem is simply a symptom that diverts attention away from marital discord, thereby serving the family system by helping it return to stable functioning. Or he should attempt to understand the themes that have been transmitted over three or four generations to see if they are part of Judy's problem.

Thus to help Ken and Marge Randolf with their daughter Judy, Pastor Coleman must decide who in the family unit to see for counseling, then what the focus of the counseling will be. In addition, he must decide the length of treatment. Should it be short-term or more long-term counseling? Finally, he also needs some way to assess the Randolf family, even if it is for purposes of referral, and then a way to make up a treatment plan that will keep him from getting lost in the family problem and keep treatment moving toward the goals that have been developed by the family.

THE NEED
FOR AN INTEGRATED MODEL

Clergy like Pastor Coleman, as well as students and trainees of family therapy, need an integrated model of family therapy that will help them make informed decisions about who to see for treatment, what to focus on in treatment, and how long to continue treatment. This integrative model must also be able to provide a map of treatment that will assist in both assessment and treatment planning.

This book is an attempt to meet this need. First, it provides an overview of basic systems theory, summarizing the history of family systems theory as well as the fundamentals of the major schools of family therapy. Second, it demonstrates how the major theories of family therapy can provide an integrative approach to assessment of couples and families. Finally, it applies this integrative model to the work of treatment planning and treatment itself. This final section employs several in-depth case studies to illustrate how the integrative treatment process works.

I hope this book provides clergy and family therapy trainees with an understanding of basic family systems concepts as well as an integrative model for providing treatment. This model should assist not only counselors in the work of family therapy but also families in the predictable life transitions, with which clergy are so intimately involved.

2

EXAMINING SEVEN
FAMILY THERAPY MODELS

Many beginning family therapists and pastoral counselors mistakenly believe that family therapy is similar to individual therapy, except that instead of working with an individual, one works with the entire family unit and gets them to talk to each other. They do not realize that family systems theory is more than a set of group techniques; it is a way of seeing and thinking. Rooted in systems theory, family systems theory insists that the counselor needs to view each person from the context of the whole unit, or system—the family. Family systems therapy has developed disparate approaches that one needs to sort out and relate to one another in order to understand and apply the therapy effectively.

ORIGINS OF FAMILY SYSTEMS THERAPY

Systems theory focuses on how interacting parts relate within a whole. It assumes that every system seeks to preserve homeostasis—a sense of equilibrium or stable functioning. Its theoretical element seeks to understand and explain how a system, whether an ecosystem or a family, regulates behavior to preserve homeostasis, especially in the face of stress. In order to understand the various perspectives within systems theory, one needs to review its history.

This theory owes much to Gregory Bateson (1972) and his associates at Palo Alto, California. In 1952 Bateson began to study communication patterns within families, and in 1954 he applied some of this communication theory to schizophrenia. He and his colleagues reasoned that a family achieves stability by feedback from its members. When the family stability is threatened, either internally or externally, the family finds a way to return to homeostasis.

For example, a couple may be experiencing severe disharmony. They do not speak to each other at meals, but seek to communicate mostly through their children. At other times, they explode into angry exchanges in the presence of their children. The children do not want this anger to continue. Then one of the children becomes ill or runs away (such behavior is called acting out). The intent of this child's acting out is to bring the parents back together, even though the child may be unaware of this intent.

Bateson and his associates analyzed specific sequences of family interactions. From this work came their now famous double-bind theory of communication—persons are caught in a no-win situation. On the one hand, a person receives an important and clear message, such as "Do this task or I will punish you." On the other hand, at a more abstract level this person receives a second message, perhaps less verbalized but equally clear, such as "Even if you do this task, I will punish you." Hence, either doing or not doing the specified action results in punishment—the pattern of the double bind from which no escape seems possible. Bateson and his colleagues believed that the impact of these double-bind messages was so powerful that continued exposure to them could produce schizophrenia.

Other important studies of the family patterns followed. Bateson's theories are generally credited with founding family systems theory. To further the studies of systems theories and family communication, Don Jackson founded the Mental Research Institute in 1959. This institute drew upon and expanded Bateson's work, and trained future leaders in family therapy like Virginia Satir, Jay Haley, and John Weakland.

CENTRAL CONCEPTS

Evolving from the foundational theories of Bateson and the Mental Research Institute, family therapists have developed a variety of theories and models. In the midst of this theoretical diversity, several important concepts of systems theory have been summarized by a number of writers including Nichols (1984), Beavers (1977), and Walsh (1982). Of these central concepts seven need to be understood before looking in more depth at the various models of family therapy.

The first central concept is a focus on the interpersonal origins of psychopathology. Early psychoanalytic theory had focused on the need for a detailed study of the individual's past, emphasizing insight into the person's intrapsychic (internal) conflicts and their genetic origins. The assumption was that when the individual achieves insight, he or she could function with much less conflict. Of little concern was the family's role in developing such conflicts or how current family relationships maintained the conflicts. In contrast, family therapy focuses on the interaction between people as the principal area for insight and change. By creating changes in both the structure and the communication of the family, one can frequently resolve problems and achieve a more appropriate sense of equilibrium. Family therapists differ, however, in how they think these changes ought to occur.

The second concept is that of the identified patient (abbreviated IP). Families often focus on or present one member as needing treatment. For example, Ms. Garcia, a sixth-grade teacher, phones the Jeffersons because their son, Justin, has frequent angry outbursts that disrupt his class in school. Ms. Garcia had referred Justin to the school counselor, who has now recommended that Jemal and Paula Jefferson, Justin's parents, seek family counseling. In the initial visit to Cynthia, a pastoral counselor, Jemal and Paula present Justin as a problem in school and want to know how Justin can be helped. "Shouldn't he receive individual counseling?" they ask Cynthia. They add that Justin has been this way since he was a toddler. Thus they label Justin as the person needing help, the identified patient.

If Cynthia is trained as an individual psychotherapist, she might undertake individual treatment of Justin. If she is trained in family systems therapy, however, she would insist that the family needs to be involved in the counseling because Justin's behavior is somehow connected to the present interaction in the Jefferson family. In the first visit, Cynthia may notice that the interaction between Jemal and Paula is strained, and she may speculate that Justin's acting out in school serves to divert attention from a troubled marriage, thus preserving the family's homeostasis.

A third concept is that a family maintains homeostasis by feedback loops that at times involve a child acting out. The acting out behavior can serve as part of a feedback loop that returns some stability to the family. Thus, in the Jefferson family, Justin's acting out brings his parents a renewed sense of togetherness as they try to get help for Justin and talk with school officials about his problems. As a result, conflict between them recedes. Here the symptom, Justin's acting out, serves the system by allowing homeostasis to return to the family.

A fourth major concept is circular causality. This notion means that because everyone in a family system is interconnected, a change in one member or subsystem affects other members and the system as a whole. Older psychoanalytic models conceived of etiology in terms of prior events that caused the symptoms in the present: linear causality. Family systems therapy helped facilitate a profound paradigm shift in moving from linear causality to circular causality. Thus in the Jefferson family, a marital problem affects Justin. When Justin acts out, the marital subsystem changes for the better. Conversely, if Justin were to stop acting out, the marital subsystem might lose its focus and change for the worse. The goal of family systems therapy is not to attempt to move back in time and understand the origin of the problem, as in the linear model, but rather to shift relationships, subsystems, and communication patterns in the present.

Related to the notions of circular causality and homeostasis, a fifth concept is that communication and patterns of communication are central in family therapy. As Watzlawick, Beavin, and Jackson (1967) point out, because it is impossible not to communicate—even not communicating is a form of communication—the careful observation of family communication patterns is crucial to family therapists. They differentiate content from process, focusing on the process by which family members communicate rather than the content that they communicate. Thus when Paula and Jemal talk about Justin's behavior problems, Cynthia, their counselor, pays careful attention to the way in which they communicate, observing that the more animated and energetic Paula becomes in her conversation, the more Jemal seems to fade away, almost as if he is out of the room.

A sixth concept is that family rules help organize family interactions. The family rarely verbalizes these rules, but they nonetheless provide expectations about family roles and actions, hence guiding family life. These rules are sometimes handed down generationally. Healthy families can adopt new structures and new rules as responses to developmental crises, whereas unhealthy families hold tenaciously to old rules and structures, thereby making the problems of the family worse. These rigid and unhealthy rules often hinder a family's work in handling normal developmental crises. For example, adolescents frequently challenge family rules and expectations. An unhealthy family cannot expand or shift these rules to incorporate adolescent issues. Second-order change—a shift in rules or ways of organizing the family—is necessary to move from one developmental stage to another.

Finally, boundaries and triangles form a seventh central idea of family systems theory. Boundaries are a necessary way of establishing hierarchies and organization within a family. They operate in three ways. First, each generation establishes boundaries to clarify who is in charge within the family. This process involves issues like making sure that grandparents do not undercut parents' disciplinary efforts and that parents do parent their children, rather than children feeling responsible for their parents, as frequently happens in alcoholic and other types of dysfunctional families. Second, boundaries separate subsystems. Each intact family has at least three subsystems: a marital subsystem that needs time apart from parenting activities, a parenting subsystem that involves parents working cooperatively as parents, and sibling subsystems that allow for sibling relationships and protect those relationships from unhealthy triangles that result when one sibling gains favored status. Third, boundaries define the way the family interacts with the outside world. The boundaries among these subsystems must be firm enough to make clear who is in charge in the family, but flexible enough to deal with ongoing changes within the family.

Triangles denote the way that a couple, when unstable, involves a third person in order to restore some stability to the relationship. For example, in the Jefferson family, the parents form a triangle with Justin to protect and stabilize an unstable dyad (the parents' relationship).

In summary, the Jefferson family illustrates the central concepts of family systems therapy. The family therapist focuses on the interpersonal components of Justin's behavior, seeking to understand the way in which his acting out preserves the family homeostasis. The family therapist works from the epistemological stance of circular causality as opposed to linear causality in attempting to understand Justin's behavior, therefore seeking to understand and observe communication patterns and family rules rather than seeing Justin as the identified patient. The family therapist strives to create a positive shift in the family to resolve the crisis. In the case of Justin, that shift might involve helping Jemal and Paula with their marriage and with their parenting skills, in order to achieve more appropriate boundaries and end the destructive triangle with Justin.

DEVELOPMENTAL THEORY

In addition to these central family systems concepts, many family therapists are informed by developmental theories that address the family life cycle. The developmental theory of Carter and McGoldrick (1980) focuses on the family life cycle. They suggest six stages of the family life cycle: (1) the unattached young adult, (2) the joining of families through marriage and the newly married couple without children, (3) the family with young children, (4) the family with adolescents, (5) launching children and moving on, and (6) the family in later life.

Each stage provides both a key emotional process that the family needs to work through and a second-order change that is necessary for the family to develop normally. For example, the couple who has been married for several years and then has children needs to accept a new generation into the family system. For this acceptance to occur, the marital system must adjust to make space for children, the couple must take on parental roles, and they must realign relationships with extended family. Problems frequently arise at a shift in one of these developmental stages in the family's history. Boundaries must adjust to accommodate change. For example, the couple who have been without children for several years and have just given birth must not only realign their relationship to make room for a child but also have sufficient boundaries to permit time for themselves as a couple.

During these developmental shifts, problems may also arise when children or adolescents inadvertently trigger unresolved issues in one or both of the parents. This triggering leads to a defensive delineation (Shapiro and Zinner 1989), in which a parent's view of a child is predominantly determined by the parent's unresolved issues. For example, a parent who has difficulty with his or her sexuality may project this difficulty onto the adolescent child and become overly involved or concerned with that adolescent child's sexuality. At one extreme, this parent may overly restrict the adolescent and begin questioning her or him intensely about dating life; at the other extreme, the parent may live vicariously through the adolescent's sexual escapades and send covert messages to the adolescent to act out sexually for the parent.

Although not a theory of family therapy per se, developmental theory provides a framework for family therapy and speaks to the predictable life stages and the crises that most families experience at those stages. It also speaks to the developmental tasks that families must accomplish in order to move through these life-stage transitions and illustrates some of the ways families can get stuck in the midst of these stages. Many family therapy models include developmental considerations in the formation of a treatment plan. Carter and McGoldrick (1980) have provided an important summary of the family life cycle. It is not in itself a model of family therapy, but most family therapy theories use it as a way of assessing where families are in terms of predictable developmental crises and tasks.

FAMILY THERAPY PARADIGMS

Most of the major models of family systems therapy accept some of the essential ingredients of systems theory but differ on the focus of family therapy. In order to understand family therapy and to work effectively from an integrated model, one must know the basic paradigms of family therapy. The integrated model presented here incorporates the following paradigms: family problem-solving therapy, structural family therapy, interactional theory, multigenerational theory, and object relations theory. In addition, cognitive theory as applied to relational problems is a relative newcomer to the field of family therapy. One must understand key concepts in each of these theories because they are the basis of the integrated model.

Family Problem-Solving Therapy

Reid (1985) developed family problem-solving therapy as a straightforward, short-term approach to family therapy that focuses on the development of family problem-solving skills. The family determines the specific problems to work on during the course of family therapy. The family therapist then works with the family using both in-session tasks and out-of-session tasks (homework) to help the family develop problem-solving abilities to deal with the problems that have brought them to treatment. Family problem-solving counselors believe that success in problem solving helps in other areas of family life. For example, if a family succeeds in solving the problem of a child's acting out in school, the family can apply this problem-solving ability to marital discord. Family problem solving is straightforward. It does not try to understand problems as pointing to deeper family issues. Rather it sees family problems simply as lack of problem-solving skills.

Jim and Nancy Hanks call the counseling center for help with Matt, their ten-year-old son, whose difficulty in school led the school guidance counselor to suggest that they get family counseling. Rather than hypothesizing how this school problem is related to underlying family problems, Joan, their counselor, works with the Hanks family on some concrete behavioral solutions to the problem. Joan helps Jim and Nancy make a behavioral contract with

Matt to resolve his school problem. After hearing from all members of the family, Jim and Nancy decide that every day Matt will bring home an assignment sheet from the teacher, and they will make sure that he does his homework. Matt wants some reward for following through, and the parents decide that if after two weeks his teacher says he has significantly improved, they will take him out for his favorite ice cream.

This is an example of straightforward problem solving using behavioral contracts. The counselor coaches the family to solve the problem during the session and to decide how they will carry out the assignment between sessions. Joan, their counselor, works with them to anticipate problems that may interfere with the assignment. If they carry out their assignment and resolve the presenting problem, therapy is usually only six to ten sessions in duration.

Frequently, however, contextual problems emerge that block problem-solving skills from developing further. Contextual problems may include a marriage that is in so much difficulty that parents cannot agree on problem-solving strategies, or an alliance between a parent and a child that subverts mutual parental problem solving. The therapist and family must deal with these contextual issues as they emerge in problem-solving therapy.

For example, after two weeks of initial success with the Hanks family, Joan noticed that Nancy Hanks was doing all the school-related work with Matt, who was becoming increasingly uncooperative. Joan reworked the problem-solving intervention by suggesting that Jim take over the assignment, and Matt became cooperative again. This contextual problem illustrates the way secondary problems may emerge through contextual difficulties in family problem-solving therapy. Counseling worked not only on the target problem brought by the family but on a contextual problem as well: Jim's lack of involvement in the parenting aspects of family life.

Structural Family Therapy

Minuchin (1974; see also Minuchin and Fishman 1981) developed structural family therapy, which focuses on the structural hierarchies of families and the ways in which families organize themselves. Structural family therapists postulate that each intact family has at least three subsystems: parental, marital, and sibling. Structural family therapists explore how the parental system (mother and father in an intact family) functions to provide strong enough boundaries to discipline the children, set developmentally appropriate boundaries, and ensure that tasks within the family are carried out. They also examine generational boundaries to see how well the family maintains boundaries between generations and to determine the influence of extended family.

The marital subsystem is of particular interest to the structural family therapist. If the marital subsystem is not nurtured or if the marriage is in serious difficulty, then the parental subsystem will have difficulty functioning. A troubled marriage can often lead to triangles or difficulties with boundaries.

For example, if marital communication breaks down, the husband or wife may form a coalition or alliance with one of the children, who then becomes the parental confidant. This coalition increasingly ostracizes the other parent and further confuses family boundaries about who is in control.

Structural theorists assert that many family problems stem from difficulties with hierarchies and boundaries. Boundaries that are too rigid may lead either to kids that cannot think for themselves or to rebellion. Boundaries that are diffuse may lead to lack of authority, confusion about who is in charge, and potential division between the parents.

The parental subsystem that does not maintain appropriate hierarchical boundaries may also lead to triangles and coalitions in which children assume a parental rule (parentification), taking on too much responsibility. For example, in an alcoholic family parents are frequently not able to maintain appropriate boundaries and function as parents due to the effects of alcoholism. As a result, one of the children may assume parental responsibilities and try to take care of the family.

When the marital subsystem is not working properly, a child may become a scapegoat, thereby providing the marital system a focus. If the couple believes that all the family problems are created by that child's acting out, then the marriage can maintain some stability by focusing on the scapegoated child. In this case the boundary between the marital subsystem and the child has not been adequate. The acting out of the child has provided an important focus for the marriage.

According to structural family theorists, healthy families have boundaries and hierarchies that are developmentally appropriate. They must be flexible enough to respond to the changing developmental needs of the family system, yet strong enough to make it clear who is in charge and to protect the marital system. This model of a healthy family is predicated on the marriage working well and on the couple working effectively as an executive subsystem, so that both husband and wife set boundaries and maintain them. It further presupposes a generational boundary that limits interference from grandparents or other extended family members.

The goal of structural family therapists is to help family members modify existing structures and boundaries or to create new structures that enable the family to solve problems more readily. The structural model assumes that problems are normal and occur as a family moves through predictable developmental stages, and that these problems are best handled by healthy family structures and developmentally appropriate boundaries.

These structural goals are accomplished by techniques such as encouraging the family to enact the problem during the session, rather than allowing the family simply to describe or talk about the problem. For example, John, a pastoral counselor, is working with Mr. and Mrs. Rodrequez and their eleven-year-old daughter Maria. Mrs. Rodrequez says to John, "I am so frustrated because Maria never listens to me." Rather than empathetically listening to her frustration or providing some parenting advice, as an individual psychotherapist might do, John encourages Mrs. Rodrequez to enact the problem by addressing her frustration to her daughter right then and there. As Mrs. Rodrequez tells Maria how frustrated she is, Maria retorts through clenched teeth, "If you would back off and give me some space, I might want to listen, but you're always on my back!"

John observes that as Maria expresses her anger, Mr. Rodrequez begins to look away, his mind seemingly elsewhere. Meanwhile the interaction between Maria and her mother begins to escalate with mutual accusations. This enactment of the problem enables John to hypothesize about the problem in structural terms, instead of simply relying on the family's verbal report of their problems. For example, John may hypothesize that Mrs. Rodrequez has an enmeshed relationship with Maria, while Mr. Rodrequez is underinvolved, perhaps not playing an active parenting role. John may also wonder if Mrs. Rodrequez is enmeshed with Maria as a way of compensating for her loneliness, which results from a distant spouse.

John can test these hypotheses by further enactments in the sessions. Thus, when the interaction between Mrs. Rodrequez and Maria escalates, John encourages Mr. Rodrequez to intervene, to take a more active role in the parenting, while encouraging Mrs. Rodrequez to take a brief vacation from her hard work of mothering.

John ends the session by assigning Mr. Rodrequez the task of taking Maria out to breakfast on her way to school, Mrs. Rodrequez the task of doing something for herself (she decides in the session to go shopping), and Mr. and Mrs. Rodrequez the task of going out to a movie together. These tasks frame the problem as structural, and both the enactment and the tasks allow John to test his hypotheses. Thus, although the family's original definition of the problem was that Maria was defiant, the scope of the problem has now been expanded to deal with Mrs. Rodrequez's overinvolvement, Mr. Rodrequez's underinvolvement, and a possible troubled marriage.

The overall goal of structural family therapy is to create structural change. Having a family enact the problem in the room enables the therapist to form hypotheses, as well as rearrange family alliances and coalitions, or rebalance over- and underinvolved parents, as John did with the Rodrequez family. Additional techniques include reframing the problem so one person does not remain the identified patient (as Maria was), and intensifying the focus, which involves increasing the volume of the therapist's message by repetition and increasing the intensity of the intervention to break through the family's resistance, their selective deafness. The technique of unbalancing aims at upsetting the present family structure and interrupting alliances by temporarily siding with different members of the family (as opposed to maintaining therapeutic neutrality), or by changing seating arrangements in the room in order to arrive at a better balance. Minuchin and Fishman (1981) outline the techniques of structural family therapy in considerable detail. These techniques serve the overall goal of restructuring the family in terms of interrupting alliances and triangles, reestablishing hierarchies so that parents are in charge, and helping shape developmentally appropriate boundaries.

Interactional Theory

Watzlawick, Beavin, and Jackson (1967) heavily influenced interactional theory, which now reflects a variety of other theories as well. In general, interactional theorists believe that interactional feedback loops often govern behavior as well as communication. Therefore, when working with couples and families, interactional therapists are especially attentive to feedback loops and the circularity of communication. For example, the more overresponsible a wife becomes, the more underresponsible her husband becomes. The less he does, the more she does, and the more she does, the less he does. This interaction is complementary and mutually reinforcing. Other examples of complementary interactions would be an assertive wife and a submissive husband, or a pursuing wife and a withdrawing husband.

Interactional theorists contrast complementary interactions with symmetrical ones, which are based more on equality. Although symmetrical relationships seem more healthy, they have their own set of difficulties. For example, if both partners are strong, and both have separate careers, arguments can easily escalate because no one backs down, whereas in a complementary relationship someone predictably backs down.

According to interactional theorists, interactional sequences maintain problems. The sequence of events in communication is maintained through punctuation (Watzlawick et al. 1967), which organizes behavioral events and helps determine how one understands content. Punctuation refers to the way a husband or wife interprets an interaction from their own perspective, and what part of the interaction they focus on. For example, Mrs. Smith insists that she pursues only because her husband withdraws and wants to spend the weekend watching football games. Mr. Smith punctuates the situation differently when he retorts in anger that he withdraws and watches football because his wife is always pursuing and nagging him for something. Such disagreements about how to punctuate the sequence of events underlie many relational difficulties.

Another problem for many couples and families is the inability to metacommunicate: to communicate about how they communicate. When the Smiths come for couples therapy, they are caught in a cycle of blame: each believes that the marriage would be fine if the other would only change. Mrs. Smith states defiantly that if her husband would only talk to her more and keep the television off, they would have a much better marriage. Mr. Smith sullenly responds that if his wife would just get off his back and give him some room to breathe, then they would have a better marriage, and he might even want to spend more time with her. Both are convinced that the other is the problem and attempt to get their counselor to change the other. Meanwhile their pursuer-distancer dance continues.

From an interactional perspective, the goal of therapy is to focus on understanding and interrupting the dance between them, framing their dance as the problem, not either of them. Therapy would also help them communicate about their style of communication and learn some more helpful ways of communication.

Interactional therapists attempt to disrupt the problem-maintaining behaviors and dysfunctional interactional styles of couples and families. Interactional theorists postulate an interactional theory of problems, assuming that what happens between people causes problems, not what happens within (intrapsychic) a person. Interactional theory does not focus on intrapsychic problems, believing that because problems are caused by what happens between people, then one brings about change by strategically shifting interactional patterns, not through intrapsychic investigation.

Others holding to the interactional or a more general communications model focus on a variety of communication issues such as helping family members speak directly to each other as opposed to focusing on the style of the interactions. For example, in working with the Lang family, the therapist, Richard, noted that whenever one of the three children spoke, Mrs. Lang interpreted the message and rephrased it to Mr. Lang. Richard observed that she seemed to be the family switchboard operator, and began to help the members of the Lang family speak directly to each other rather than through Mrs. Lang.

Additional communication goals might include helping each person in the family use "I" statements as opposed to "you" or "we" statements. Mrs. Lang tended to use "we" instead of "I" because she assumed that she spoke for the entire family unit. Richard needed to confront Mrs. Lang about this behavior so other family members could speak for themselves. In contrast, Mr. Lang, when pushed, used attacking "you" statements, such as "You make me so angry that I can't concentrate at work." Richard coached him to make direct "I" statements to the person with whom he was angry, thereby owning and taking responsibility for his anger.

Counseling frequently involves not only the therapeutic interruption of family interactions but some specific skill training in listening, in resolving conflict, and in assertiveness so people can learn to ask directly to have their needs met. Although all interactional therapists agree that change occurs as the interactions between people change, not all agree on the therapist's role in accomplishing that change. Some hold that change occurs through straightforward interventions, such as interpretations that lead to insight, direct skill building in communications, or helping people understand and change their interactional dance.

Those from the strategic school of interactional family therapy take a different tack. They suggest that although straightforward interventions may work, more often than not they fail. Strategic therapists argue that straightforward advice too often simply resembles the sort of advice that couples give each other and receive from well-meaning family and friends, and such advice rarely produces change. To get more powerful leverage, they believe strategic interventions are needed.

One paradoxical strategic intervention is called prescribing the symptom. For example, a counselor working with a couple caught in the pursuer-distancer dance may coach the pursuer to pursue more passionately, thereby changing the context of the behavior and the pattern of interaction. The Milan group (an influential family therapy group in Milan, Italy) uses a form of prescription called positive connotation. For instance, an adolescent's acting out is relabeled as a wonderful sacrifice to give parents a focus, thereby preserving the marriage as well as the family. This relabeling may encourage the adolescent to continue making the heroic sacrifice to help stabilize the family.

Although scholars debate the efficacy of these types of interventions because families seem manipulated into changing, many family therapists argue that straightforward interventions work well with compliant clients, but that with noncompliant clients more paradoxical techniques are necessary to produce change. Paradoxical techniques resemble the reverse psychology that parents often try on their children. For example, instead of asking a couple to stop fighting, a paradoxical technique would be to recommend they fight even more, since it is their only means of intimacy. All do agree, however, that change occurs as a response to changed interactions.

Cognitive Therapy

As originally developed by Beck (1976, 1988) and by Ellis (1976), cognitive therapy focuses on the way in which cognitive distortions produce emotional problems. Cognitive distortions refer to beliefs people hold about the meaning of events or communication. These beliefs or cognitions may distort what is actually said. For example, Susan believes that her worth as a bookkeeper will be proved by a perfect job review. When her supervisor notes several areas for improvement, she feels devastated. Susan's belief that she needs a perfect job review keeps her from seeing her review as basically positive. This theory has been applied predominantly to depression and anxiety disorders, although Beck (1988) has expanded the theory to apply to relational problems. It focuses on how cognitive distortions twist communication in couples and families, and seeks to understand and correct these distortions, thus enabling communication to proceed more smoothly.

Cognitive marriage and family therapy also focuses on general thinking styles, on underlying beliefs about the nature of marital and family relationships. Cognitive theory aims at helping the couple or family identify the "cognitive grid" (Beck, 1988) that each member uses to interpret communication, in addition to recognizing personal beliefs that hinder the relationship. This cognitive grid refers to core beliefs that people hold to about relationships. For example, if a husband believes that proof of love and of a good relationship is mind reading, that his wife should instinctively know his needs, then each time she does not respond to his unspoken needs he will feel unloved. Only as these beliefs are identified and changed can the relational difficulties be ameliorated.

In general, then, cognitively oriented marriage and family counselors work to understand people's beliefs about relationships, which are often not verbalized. Beck (1988) lists a number of these beliefs, including mind reading ("if you really loved me you would know what I want without my having to ask"); all-or-nothing thinking ("if you fail in one area you really do not love me"); catastrophizing, which turns the normal irritants of life into catastrophes ("if you don't do your homework you'll flunk out and never get a good job"); arbitrary inference, where one spouse may jump to a conclusion that does not seem to have a basis in reality ("he's doing this just to irritate me"); and tunnel vision, in which one sees only data that fit one's beliefs about the other and ignores what does not. Because these cognitive distortions happen automatically, people are frequently not aware of how they distort communication through these cognitive grids.

More specifically, cognitive couples therapy investigates these cognitive distortions in regard to specific cycles of interaction between people, and then uses them to help couples understand how they distort communications. For example, Rob and Karen reported in a session that they had had a difficult week and were feeling somewhat hopeless about the future of their marriage. Karen said that three days ago she had come home quite excited about her latest job review and looked forward to sharing it with Rob. But Rob seemed distant and disinterested and so she withdrew, feeling angry and resentful, and thought to herself, "Rob really doesn't want me to be successful at work; he is interested only in his own life and in his own career."

Rob protested to the counselor that the same day had been difficult for him, and he had come home with a splitting headache. He recalled that as Karen talked he was wishing that he could lie down, but did not say that to Karen; instead he tried to pretend that he was interested and paying attention. As Karen backed away and became angry, Rob concluded she would never be sensitive to his needs because she was tied up in her own career. He remembered saying to himself, "I wish I had a wife who would know what I need without my having to ask. Karen will never be sensitive to my needs."

A cognitive therapist would help Karen and Rob sort out their cognitive distortions and counterproductive thinking styles. The therapist must help Karen see her arbitrary inferences, which she needed to check out in reality. She needs help understanding the downward spiral of her beliefs, which often results in her ending up being distant and angry. Rob needs help understanding and challenging his expectations that his wife be able to read his mind, as well as the way in which his arbitrary inferences lead him through a downward spiral of beliefs. Together, Karen and Rob would then understand the cyclical interaction of their belief system that inevitably leaves them distant and angry.

Cognitively oriented marriage and family therapists begin by assessing the cognitive profile of both partners, perhaps using some standardized testing instruments as well as the couple's own description of their beliefs and the therapist's observations. Clients are taught to monitor in written form their dysfunctional thoughts and the emotions such thoughts arouse. They are then taught to challenge their cognitive distortions with what cognitive therapists refer to as rational statements. These are statements that are more reality oriented.

For example, in the midst of a counseling session, Mary states reluctantly, "If I let my guard down and trust Russ again, I just know that he will stop working on the relationship and hurt me again." Her counselor helps Mary see this as an overgeneralization, which is one type of cognitive distortion. Her counselor encourages her to make a rational restatement: "I really have no evidence to support this feeling. Perhaps letting down my defenses might enable Russ to get closer to me." By progressively challenging cognitive distortions, the couple can move from a negative and pessimistic view to a more positive and optimistic view of the relationship and its future. This more positive view then allows communication to improve and greater intimacy to emerge. Primary techniques include tracking cognitive distortions by attempting to understand the beliefs behind communication, challenging those distortions, and making behavioral changes that interrupt those distortions.

Multigenerational Theory

Bowen (1978) developed multigenerational theory, which focuses on how families transmit themes and patterns over generations. Bowen's theory has been expanded by writers like Friedman (1985), Brown (1991), Roberto (1992), and Framo (1992). Key concepts in this theory include multigenerational transmission, triangulation, and differentiation of self.

Multigenerational transmission is the transference of marital patterns, ways of being in relationship, and even psychopathology over several generations in a family. For example, one can usually trace alcoholism and incest over at least three generations.

In the Bible the family of Abraham serves as an example of how patterns of parenting emerge over several generations. Abraham was involved in several intense family triangles. One triangle began with Abraham and Sarah's difficulty conceiving, which resulted in Abraham using Sarah's servant Hagar to produce a son (Ishmael). This situation caused a triangle between Abraham, Sarah, and Hagar. When Sarah finally conceived and gave birth to Isaac, the issue intensified to include two siblings. The painful outcome of this triangle was that Hagar and Ishmael were sent away.

Abraham's son Isaac eventually married Rebekah, and their marriage produced twins: Jacob and Esau. These twins both became part of triangles—Isaac's favorite child was Esau, while Rebekah favored Jacob—which exacerbated their sibling rivalry. The eventual outcome of this rivalry was that Jacob stole his brother's birthright, through a cunning maneuver that Rebekah devised. As a result of this deception and the stolen birthright, Jacob had to flee from his brother's rage.

Later, when Jacob had his own family, he favored his son Joseph. This favoritism resulted in yet another generation with intense sibling rivalry and triangulation, and Joseph's brothers sold him into slavery.

This biblical story illustrates the concept of multigenerational transmission, with three generations each having triangulation, sibling rivalry, covert parental coalitions, parental division, scapegoating, and one child being played against another. Each generation seemed to repeat blindly the same mistakes with tragic consequences. Multigenerational transmission brings to mind the verse, "punishing children for the iniquity of parents" (Exodus 20:5).

Bowen (1978) postulated that when anxiety arises in a relationship, people frequently create triangles in order to diffuse that anxiety and to stabilize the relationship. Thus one could postulate that because Isaac and Rebekah's marriage was shaky, they formed triangles with their twins: Rebekah and Jacob against Isaac (and Esau), and Isaac and Esau against Rebekah (and Jacob). Although these triangles have dangerous implications, they do serve to stabilize marital relationships by refocusing the anxiety and conflict.

Several types of triangulation exist. Parents can align against a child; one family member can be a type of shuttle running back and forth between two other family members; or one parent and a child can form a triangle against the other parent. Some parents use one child as a marriage counselor. At other times one child becomes a substitute spouse, the confidant of a spouse. Another family can scapegoat one child as the family problem, thereby not having to look at any other family problems. These triangles function to contain anxiety and conflict in families and stabilize relationships.

The second key concept of multigenerational theory is differentiation of self: the ability to maintain relationship to one's family of origin by being oneself. It is measured along a continuum, with cutoff on one extreme and enmeshment on the other. Thus, the differentiated adult does not simply cut off or rarely have contact with her or his family of origin, but can be with them without becoming enmeshed with them. One can maintain a sense of nonanxious presence (see Friedman 1985, 208, 209) with one's family of origin; one does not have to diffuse the anxiety by either cutting off or enmeshing. The differentiated person is nonreactive, whereas the nondifferentiated person becomes reactive in times of anxiety and stress, and loses objectivity and the ability to stay outside the reactive cycles. Family health is proportional to the level of differentiation of self of each person in the marital system.

A multigenerational therapist begins with a genogram, a diagram of the family that helps clients understand themselves from the vantage point of at least three generations. A genogram reveals significant triangles, cutoffs, and multigenerational themes and patterns.

The goal of therapy is not simply insight but change. Change is accomplished largely by going-home exercises, with the therapist acting as coach to help facilitate differentiation and nonanxious presence. Going-home exercises involve understanding the predictable interactional cycles, family rules, and triangles that manifest themselves routinely during family get-togethers. A plan of action is then formulated to enable the person to be nonreactive, and to make specific changes in these family interactions (rather than working out the changes in one's head, as in insight oriented therapies). The goal is not to change others in the family, but to change how one responds to the family, by becoming less reactive.

Nick and Martha made an appointment for marriage counseling. In their first session with Gary, a pastoral counselor, Martha said that they had difficulty communicating. Gary asked them to be more specific about the nature of their communication problem, and their responses made clear to Gary that they had developed a dance: Martha would pursue and Nick would distance. As Martha tearfully put it: "I'm so tired of trying. Each time I ask Nick if we can turn off the TV and talk, or even go for a walk, he says he has something to do. It really hurts to feel that he never wants to talk with me." As soon as the words were out of her mouth, Nick exploded. "She is always exaggerating. She just expects too much from me, so no matter how much I talk with her it is never enough."

When Gary encouraged them to talk about their families of origin, it became clear that Martha was cut off from her family of origin: she saw them only occasionally and rarely talked with her father. As she described her relationship with her father she began to cry. "I tried so hard to build a relationship with my father, but it almost seemed that I didn't exist to him because I wasn't a boy." By contrast, Nick had grown up in a family that he described as enmeshed and suffocating, where he felt his mother's control constantly. "You couldn't breathe in my family. I couldn't wait to go to college and get away from them." He added insightfully, "You know, I hate to admit it, but now that we're talking about this, when Martha is always trying to get me to talk, it feels like my mother is trying to control me all over again. She was constantly telling me to talk to her more."

Gary worked with Nick and Martha to help them understand the influence their respective families had on them as individuals and as a couple. Understanding the importance of multigenerational themes, Gary realized that they needed to work on going home, on reengaging their families of origin and making some changes there. Nick needed to learn to be with his family non-anxiously and nonreactively, without being controlled by his mother or anyone else in the family. As he made some changes in his family of origin, he slowly became stronger in the marriage and did not have to distance from Martha. For her part Martha needed to learn to connect more with her family of origin, and Gary coached her on some small steps in building a relationship with her father. Although this was slow and difficult work for Martha, the more progress she made, the more her need to be overly close with Nick began to decrease, and the less she pursued him.

Object Relations Theory

In developing object relations family therapy, the Scharffs (1987, 1989, 1991) and Slipp (1984, 1988) borrowed heavily from the work of object relations theorists like Klein, Fairbairn, and Dicks. Object relations theorists see families as a system of sets of relationships, including the internalized object relations of each of its members.

Although its name seems misleading, object relations theory is concerned with the way one internalizes early primary relationships and self-images. These internalized relationships or persons form a map or model that can greatly influence spouse selection and relational dynamics. Problems in relationships result primarily from unconscious attempts to reenact, externalize, or master intrapsychic conflicts originating in one's family of origin. For example, if a woman had a domineering father and unconsciously internalizes his image, she may marry a domineering husband and try to work through her conflicts with her father in the marital relationship. One task, then, of object relations family therapy is to attempt to understand the internalized objects of each of the family members, and to understand the present in the light of one's inner object world and one's unconscious attempts to modify close relationships to fit internal role models. This is based on the object relations premise that one's capacity to function as a friend, lover, spouse, and parent is largely a consequence of one's childhood relationships with one's parents, and the way in which one internalized those relationships.

Problems occur in families largely through projective identification: one identifies a child or spouse as holding an unwanted or longed-for part of the other. For example, a parent who has not appropriately resolved his or her own sexual problems projects this unwanted sexual part of the self onto the child, who is seen as too interested in sex or too interested in members of the opposite sex. This projection may result on the other hand in parents being overly strict and restrictive, or on the other hand in their living vicariously through their child's sexual escapades.

Problems may also occur as the result of inadequate separation and individuation on the part of the parents. Mahler, Pine, and Bergman (1975) and other developmental psychologists have described in detail the way in which infants begin the work of separation from their mother and individuation that leads to the formation of a self. For example, if a mother has had difficulty separating from her own mother, then she may have difficulty allowing her own children to separate from her. Along the same lines, if a father has had difficulty individuating from his own family (i.e., has not formed a separate self), then he may experience difficulty if his children form values and identities significantly different from his own.

Anthony Provine, a husband, father of three boys, and an impeccably dressed executive, erupted in the midst of a family session: "I never thought parenting would be like this. I always did whatever my parents told me, or there would have been hell to pay. Mike [his fourteen-year-old son] does whatever he damn well pleases. Look at him—with that long hair, earring, and raunchy T-shirt—does he look like my son? After all my work, I don't think he holds any of my values or beliefs. I can't live with it anymore." He then tried to fight back the tears of hurt and frustration.

Carol, the family therapist, began softly to question him about his own relationship with his father. At first, Anthony insisted it was a great relationship. Then he began to reflect more introspectively. "You know, it always had to be my father's way. I wanted to major in art, but he told me in no uncertain terms that if I didn't become a business major, he wouldn't pay a dime toward my college education. I always had the feeling that if I was not exactly what he wanted me to be, he would never accept me." Carol was able to work with Anthony, while Mike listened intently, and help him see that Mike's attempt to individuate from him was something that he had not been able to work out with his own father.

The goal of object relations family therapy is not to resolve symptoms but to help the family provide an adequate holding environment (a safe nurturing place with appropriate boundaries and ample support) that allows for the developmental needs of its members, and to allow individual family members to improve their ability to differentiate.

The therapeutic relationship offers a safe place for the family, a holding environment, where new understandings and family styles can develop. It also allows for the sorting out and working through of defense mechanisms like projective identifications, in which one family member projects an unwanted aspect of him- or herself on another family member and attacks it in that family member, and splitting, in which one sees everything, people included, in rigid black-and-white categories and tolerates no ambivalence.

The Rodger family came for counseling because of their sixteen-year-old daughter Jennifer. Mrs. Rodger summarized the problem through clenched teeth when David, their pastoral counselor, asked what brought them to counseling. She blurted out, "She [pointing angrily at Jennifer] has no morals. We didn't raise her to act like a tramp." Portraying Jennifer as the identified patient, Mrs. Rodger claimed that they had found out that Jennifer was sexually involved with her boyfriend.

As the therapy moved forward, David's attempt to normalize Jennifer's sexual interest by pointing out that it was age appropriate further enraged the Rodgers. They retorted that they had raised Jennifer to be different, and had taught her Christian values. Efforts to help Mrs. Rodger step back and give Jennifer some freedom and trust met with similar resistance.

Over time, however, as the Rodgers were able to trust their counselor, they could talk about their struggles in their families of origin. Mrs. Rodger had been in an enmeshed relationship with her mother and had been very distant from her father, particularly as a teenager. She tearfully admitted, "I made a lot of mistakes when I was Jennifer's age." She cried quietly for a few moments and then added, "I guess I always hoped I could keep Jennifer from making the same mistakes I made." She then explained that she had gone through a time of sexual acting out when she was Jennifer's age that had left her with many emotional scars. She acknowledged that at this point she and her husband had little sexual activity.

While remaining empathically attuned to Mrs. Rodger, David was able to hypothesize that the Rodgers had formed a defensive delineation (Shapiro and Zinner 1989). Mrs. Rodger was projecting her unresolved issues with sex and with her mother onto Jennifer. At the same time Mr. Rodger was projecting his anger over the lack of sex within the marriage onto Jennifer, thereby preserving the marital homeostasis. Only as Mrs. Rodger began to work on her own issues, and as the couple talked about what was going on between them, could they withdraw the projection. Over time Jennifer stopped acting out sexually.

THE NEED FOR INTEGRATION

Family therapy students are often exposed to all these schools of thought in their first marriage and family therapy course. It may seem obvious to them that all these theories have some truth in them. But they often do not learn to make informed decisions regarding which approach to use, or how systematically and thoughtfully to integrate the theories. As a result, they frequently either apply the same theory to all cases or use a fragmented eclecticism. They lack an integrative approach to assessment and to treatment planning.

3

MAPPING
EACH THEORY'S
DEEP STRUCTURES

A logical place to begin developing an integrative model of family therapy is with the process of assessment. Beginning family therapists have usually taken a survey course, which reviews the major theories of family therapy (summarized in chap. 2). Thus most novice therapists are familiar with the major theories of change, of psychopathology, and of family mental health. They may even have had the opportunity to observe a master family therapist at a national training conference. Armed with this information, beginning family therapists have their initial session with a family.

For example, Amy, a beginning family therapist, had the basic introductory courses in family therapy and some basic supervision of her counseling work. Her first family therapy session was with the Sanchez family. In the initial phone conversation Mrs. Sanchez reported that her oldest son Juan had been in many fights at school and seemed angry much of the time. She wondered if Amy would see Juan for individual counseling in order to help him with his anger. Amy responded that she would like everyone living at home to come to the first session. Mr. and Mrs. Sanchez, Juan, and his three younger sisters came to the session.

As Amy began the session, she observed that Juan sat sullenly in a corner of the room. Mr. and Mrs. Sanchez sat across from each other with some discomfort, while Juan's three younger sisters sat on the couch together, appearing confused as to why they were there. After trying to get acquainted with the family and helping them feel at ease, Amy asked each person why they thought they had been invited to the session. Juan's two younger sisters were confused about why they were there, but Mr. and Mrs. Sanchez and Julie, the oldest sister, all agreed that the problem was Juan, and that if he would stop being so hostile, the family would be much happier. Juan retorted that he was there only because his parents forced him to come, and that they had the problem. "Now what!" thought Amy nervously. "What do I do next? How do I determine what the problem really is?"

Some would tell Amy that she should begin by drawing a genogram to determine some of the patterns transmitted over several generations, and then

35

examine the level of differentiation of each member of the family, paying particular attention to how Mr. and Mrs. Sanchez differentiated from their own families.

Others would say that she must assess the family structure in terms of boundaries and hierarchies and the way the family handles power, as well as the state of the marriage. Those from this structural perspective would urge Amy to help restructure the family.

Still others would urge Amy to help the family with their problem-solving skills and attempt to arrive at a behavioral contract with Juan that would seek to reinforce other behaviors while extingishing his angry behavior.

Interactionalists would suggest that Amy should first assess how the family communicates and their patterns of communication. By assessing these patterns Amy could help the family to cope differently with Juan's problem.

Those from the cognitive school would advise that assessment focus on understanding the cognitive distortions and irrational belief systems manifest in the family interactions. Their focus would be to form a cognitive profile of each member of the family, understanding key irrational beliefs that distort communication and assessing the interplay between cognitions and communication.

Finally, those from the object relations school of thought would want Amy to assess how well the family provides a holding environment for its members, and how well family members handle separation and individuation. In addition, they would encourage Amy in her assessment to look for possible defensive delineations, places where one or both of the parents project onto Juan unresolved issues in their own developmental histories, or project unresolved anger on him to act out for them.

With all this advice ringing in her ears, Amy would likely feel more overwhelmed than helped in her attempt to make a thorough assessment. Like many beginning family therapists, she would probably have difficulty knowing where to start.

MODELS OF FAMILY HEALTH

If Amy looks to the literature on family health for additional help in her attempt to make an assessment, she may again feel overwhelmed by the data. Four models of family health are common in the literature: those of Offer and Sabshin (1974), Olson, Russell, and Sprenkle (1989), Beavers (1977), and McMaster (Walsh, 1988).

Writing about mental health in general, Offer and Sabshin (1974), suggest four ways of understanding health.

1. Normality as health. Health is the absence of pathology or disability. Thus, in regard to family life, this theory suggests that the healthy family is one with no evidence of gross pathology or problems.

2. Normality as utopia. This idea has its roots in the psychoanalytic notion that health is integration, which results in optimal functioning or in self-actualization in which one is able to reach one's full potential. Applied to family life this notion means that the ideal family promotes the self-actualization of each of its members.
3. Normality as a statistical average. This view postulates that one can measure normality statistically on a bell-shaped curve. The middle range is normal and both extremes are deviant. The healthy or normal family is simply the average family, as established empirically.
4. The view of normality as process sees normal behavior as the result of interacting systems that change over time. This allows for flexible interactions so that developmental issues can be worked through appropriately. Family health is related to how well families adapt to the changing developmental needs of family members, while allowing for growth and maintenance.

Olson, Russell, and Sprenkle (1989) write specifically about the task of family assessment. They propound a circumplex model of family assessment, which seeks to measure three essential traits of healthy families: cohesion, adaptability, and communication. Cohesion has four levels, ranging from disengaged (very low cohesion), to separated (low to moderate cohesion), to connected (moderate to high cohesion), to enmeshed (very high cohesion). Adaptability is also measured on four levels, ranging from rigid (very low adaptability), to structured (low to moderate adaptability), to flexible (moderate to high adaptability), to chaotic (extremely high adaptability). Finally, communication is critical for facilitating families to move toward healthier cohesion and adaptability. One can employ the circumplex model to build a map of different types of marriages and families, using the measures of cohesion and adaptability. From this map Olson, Russell, and Sprenkle derive a series of hypotheses about healthy families.

Beavers (1977) writes about family health from the vantage point of a major research study. On the basis of his research he outlines three types of families: severely dysfunctional, mid-range, and healthy, and then he describes characteristics of each type. Healthy families have eight characteristics.

1. A systems orientation. Family members understand that they are parts of systems, and any action that they take affects other members of the family.
2. Boundary issues. The healthy family has developmentally appropriate boundaries that are neither too rigid nor too flexible, but adapt in response to the changing developmental needs of the family.
3. Contextual clarity. In healthy families it is clear to whom communication is addressed, and nonverbal messages are congruent with verbal messages.

4. Power issues. Healthy families have a balance of power. Parental coalitions are generally egalitarian and do not rely on coercive power.
5. Autonomy. Healthy families encourage autonomy, and parenting is done with the vision of preparing children to leave and begin their own lives.
6. Affective issues. Healthy families exhibit a warm, optimistic feeling; the members are involved with each other, and each is interested in what the other has to say. Healthy families both allow and resolve conflict.
7. Negotiation and task performance. Healthy families can organize themselves to respond to a task, negotiate differences, and carry out the task.
8. Transcendent values. Healthy families believe in something beyond themselves that allows them to deal with basic existential questions, including issues of loss. The transcendent values vary, from religion to political stances.

Beavers examines how these variables manifest themselves in healthy families, and compares these families to mid-range families and dysfunctional families. He talks about how different disorders can arise from different types of families.

The McMaster model of family functioning and family health (see Walsh 1988) assesses families in terms of six dimensions.

1. Family problem solving. Healthy families are able to move through a sequence of steps in order to solve a variety of family problems, including affective problems, which relate to emotions or feelings, and instrumental problems, which are mechanical in nature, such as provision of money, food, and shelter.
2. Communication. Healthy families communicate clearly and directly as opposed to obscurely and indirectly. Communication is also evaluated in terms of affective issues and instrumental issues.
3. Affective responsiveness. Families have a potential range of affective responses to various stimuli. One can evaluate two aspects of affective responses: the range of feelings that the family experiences, and the emotion's compatibility with the situation.
4. Affective involvement. Families value and display interest in the activities of various members to differing degrees, ranging from lack of involvement to symbiotic involvement; healthy families practice empathic involvement where families are sensitive to each other's needs.
5. Roles. In this model's definition, roles are repetitive patterns of behavior that enable family members to fulfill family functions. Five important family functions are: provision of resources, nurturance and support, adult sexual gratification, personal development, and the basic maintenance and management of the family system that helps the family run

properly. Healthy families fulfill these necessary family functions by appropriate allocation of roles.

6. Behavior control. This is defined as the pattern a family adopts for handling physically dangerous situations, situations where psychobiological needs (such as eating, drinking, or sex) must be met or expressed, and situations involving interpersonal socializing both inside and outside the family. This model describes four types of behavior control: rigid, flexible, laissez-faire, and chaotic. Flexible behavior control is the most healthy.

Although these theorists have provided some helpful and interesting schemas for understanding methods of assessing family health, it still remains difficult to move from theory to practice. For example, after carefully studying various theories of assessment, Amy, the beginning family therapist, still has to decide how to treat the Sanchez family. Simply assessing where the family is in terms of cohesion and adaptability, or knowing how they compare on Beavers's scale of healthy family functioning, or even if they are a healthy, mid-range, or severely dysfunctional family may not help one to decide how to work with the family to resolve the problems that brought them to treatment.

Many family counselors have no clear guidelines for how to make assessments, yet they must counsel families with a wide assortment of problems. If they have a model for assessment, it is often limited to the model of family therapy in which they have been trained; or perhaps they have some limited training in one of the models of family health and family assessment. For example, if one has received training in structural family therapy, then one will assess according to the theory of structural family therapy. Thus the therapist will assess the family's structure in terms of how boundaries are set, in terms of hierarchies, and in terms of how the family handles power. Or one trained in a Bowenian model of family therapy will assess that the problem is related to a multigenerational theme, such as a cutoff.

The danger is that one's theory becomes a cognitive frame that limits and determines what one can see. For example, one trained in structural family therapy tends to see all family problems as manifestations of structural problems. Thus one may overlook other sources of the problems (e.g., interactional, cognitive, multigenerational) and thereby limit the success of treatment.

INTEGRATIVE ASSESSMENT

An integrative approach to family therapy proposes a straightforward and systematic approach to assessment. Rather than view the couple or family's problem through the lens of a single treatment modality, one moves through a series of steps in order to arrive at an adequate assessment of the problem.

This approach allows for an unfolding of the problem, ideally without imposing the counselor's frame upon the couple. It begins with the simplest and most obvious level, that of problem solving, and then moves sequentially through other stages (see diagram 1). Assessment at each level ought to lead either to resolution of the problem or to assessment at another level.

For example, Debra called a counseling center, explaining over the phone that her marriage was in trouble and that she and her husband Paul were having trouble communicating. She requested an appointment with a counselor as soon as possible. When Ed, a marriage and family counselor, saw them for an initial session later that week, Debra began by saying that she did not know how long she could stay in the marriage because she could no longer tolerate Paul's long hours as a middle manager with a local corporation. Paul routinely worked twelve-hour days and would come home exhausted, wanting only to read the newspaper, watch the news on television, and then fall asleep. Paul responded calmly that he knew things had to change and that work would soon settle down and he would have more time to spend communicating. Debra exploded. "You've been saying that for the last five years and things never get better! I think you really just don't want to spend time with me." She started to cry, and Paul looked away without saying a word. With that introduction Ed felt pressured to get a handle on what was going on between them and attempt to form at least a preliminary assessment and a working hypothesis.

Preliminary Questions and Considerations

As part of an integrative assessment, Ed must ask some preliminary questions, such as, Why now? Why have Debra and Paul picked this time to begin counseling, rather than two months ago, or two weeks ago? What has happened to cause one of them, in this case Debra, to request an appointment as soon as possible? As Ed explored questions with the couple, he realized that several events had prompted the emergency. First, they had had an intense fight last week, which resulted in days of silence, with Paul finally vowing that if things did not change he would move out. Second, one of Paul's friends had just gone through a divorce, and Debra worried about how it would influence Paul. Ed realized that although their relationship had been rocky for some time, Debra had recently begun to fear losing Paul.

Ed also wondered why they chose this counseling center. When he asked them, they said that a friend had had therapy at the center and recommended it highly. They implied both that this was a last-ditch effort to save the marriage, and that they had high expectations of the marriage counseling.

Another question Ed asked them was when their marital trouble began. They had been married for six years, and Ed inquired about what had attracted them to each other, the early years of the marriage, the strengths of the marriage, and when the marriage started to become problematic. For the first time in the session, both Paul and Debra relaxed noticeably as they began discussing some of the strengths of the relationship, and they recalled with some humor what had attracted them to each other. Together they were able to recognize that the first signs of trouble occurred three years ago, when Debra began to advance rapidly as an investment broker, while Paul remained somewhat stagnant in his accounting firm. This discrepancy in career movement exacerbated a pattern that had surfaced at times in their relationship: Debra pursued and pushed Paul to take more initiative to get his career moving.

Finally, in terms of the family life cycle, Ed assessed Paul and Debra as being in the second stage described by Carter and McGoldrick (1980): the couple without children. He began to wonder how they had dealt with their own issues of separation, individuation, and differentiation of self. He filed away this question as one to deal with later in the assessment procedure.

This example shows some of the basic assessment questions asked in the first interview. They include why now, what is the problem that has brought them for counseling, why did they choose this counseling center, how long has the problem been occurring, when did it start occurring, and what are the strengths in the marriage or family. From responses to these questions one forms a preliminary hypothesis, and from this position the counselor is ready to begin moving through the stages outlined on the assessment grid (diagram 1). This assessment grid is intended to clearly display the major issues that family assessment must touch on.

Problem-Solving Assessment

Assessment begins with problem solving, which is the simplest level. The counselor must first identify the problem that has brought the couple or family in for counseling. This may not be as easy as it sounds. Many couples describe rather vaguely what has brought them in for counseling. Simply stating that they need better communication skills or need to feel closer does not provide the counselor with much information. The counselor must work hard to help the couple or family state in concrete terms what has brought them to counseling, and then help them set goals that they both agree would address the problem that caused them to come to counseling in the first place.

For example, in counseling Debra and Paul, Ed had to work to help them state the problem more concretely. If Ed simply agreed that the problem was how Paul could cut down on the hours that he was working, therapy would probably fail, after many well-intentioned efforts on Paul's part to slow down his schedule.

As they talked about the problem in the first session, Paul acknowledged, "I feel that whatever I do will make Debra angry! If I cut back on my hours she will feel that I'm not getting ahead in my career and will be disappointed

DIAGRAM 1
Integrative Assessment Model

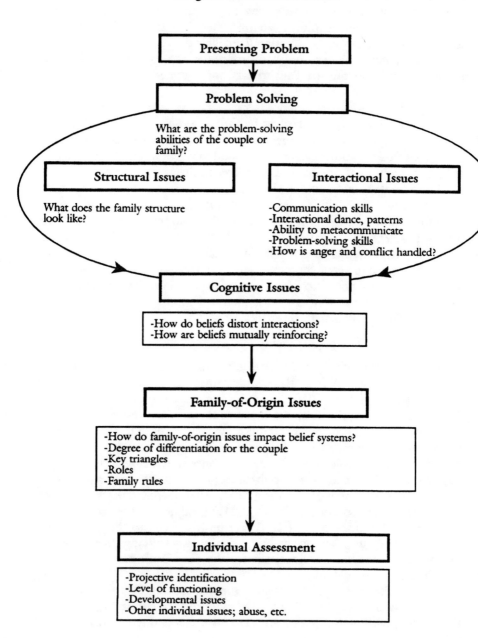

in me. If I keep working the hours that I'm working she complains that I'm never home and am trying to avoid her. What am I supposed to do?"

Framing the problem in a way that both Paul and Debra can accept is essential. Ed suggested, "It sounds like both of you are unhappy with how the marriage is going. One of the problems I'm hearing is that you are both having difficulty finding quality time together. Does that sound right?" Both Paul and Debra agreed with that initial summary of the problem. So far so good: both accepted a definition of the problem that was nonblaming and nonjudgmental.

After giving a preliminary definition of the problem that the couple accepts, the counselor must assess the couple's problem-solving skills. This assessment involves how the couple solves or attempts to solve problems together, and whether their impasse with the problem that they brought to the first session is abnormal. Are they usually good at problem solving, and is the presenting problem simply an unusual one? Or does the couple have several toxic or repetitive problems in their relationship that their problem-solving skills do not seem to affect? Perhaps the couple has little problem-solving skill and needs a great deal of skill training in order to move forward. These are important questions to resolve during the problem-solving stage.

Discussion with the couple will answer some of these questions. But the beginning counselor must not be seduced into simply talking about the problem. This mistake is easy to make. One can spend a great deal of time talking about the problem under the guise of gathering information, without seeing the couple in action. At an early point in the process, the counselor must convince the couple to talk to each other about the problem and thereby enact it. Then the counselor can more adequately see their problem-solving abilities.

For example, toward the end of the initial session Ed asked Paul and Debra to talk to each other about how they could spend more quality time together. They began rather awkwardly, but within several minutes Debra began to push Paul, while Paul began to back down and withdraw from her suggestions. When Ed attempted to help with their problem solving, the situation did not improve much. Thus Ed gained important information: he realized that Debra and Paul had few problem-solving skills, at least in some significant areas of their marriage.

As an initial part of his assessment he began to wonder why. Both were well-spoken, intelligent adults with good jobs and good educations; they had good problem-solving skills in their careers. Within the marriage, however, these problem-solving skills did not work. Ed realized that they would probably not make much progress on the problem-solving front. As the next level of assessment he asked himself what kept this intelligent couple from solving problems effectively.

Interactional Assessment

The next step in integrative assessment is to look at how counterproductive interactional cycles affect problem solving. One may assess a variety of interactional sequences at this level.

Symmetrical interactions occur when two people have similar styles. For example, if both husband and wife are domineering and will not back down, interactions between them tend to escalate to a crescendo, offering no opportunity to resolve the issue.

In complementary interactional sequences the behavior or response of one party fits that of the other party. For example, if a husband is domineering and his wife is submissive, they have a complementary interaction, which will probably stay balanced. If a wife yells and gets hysterical, while her husband remains calm and passive, they too have a complementary interaction. These complementary interactions tend to maintain homeostasis.

Two well-known examples of complementary interactions are the pursuer-distancer interaction and the codependent-addict interaction.

In the pursuer-distancer dance, one person pursues while the other distances. One spouse or parent constantly says "we need to talk more" or "we must spend more time together," while the other responds "maybe later" or "I'm too busy." Both stay frustrated and insist that the other is the problem. The way they punctuate this interaction blocks any type of self-focus, perpetuating the cycle of blaming the other, which in turn prevents any constructive problem solving.

In the codependent-addict relationship, one person (the codependent) derives satisfaction from taking care of the other (usually an alcoholic or substance abuser) in a counterproductive manner. For example, a woman married to an alcoholic would not confront his drinking or its effect on the family, but would make excuses and bail her husband out of difficult situations (e.g., by calling up his boss and saying he was sick when he was simply hung over from drinking the night before). Her behavior enabled him to continue drinking without facing the consequences of his behavior. He on the other hand would continue to drink, relying on his wife to keep him from facing the consequences of his behavior.

Parents occasionally get into this pattern with their adolescents. Instead of holding them responsible and helping them face the consequences of their behavior, they may cover for them in school, hence enabling their irresponsible behavior to continue.

To return to Debra and Paul: as Ed attempted to assess their interactional style, he soon recognized that this couple was engaged in a pursuer-distancer dance. The more Debra pursued, the more Paul distanced. As a result their relationship was complementary, and homeostasis was maintained. Both remained frustrated and stalemated, with nothing changing in the relationship.

Ed knew that it would be difficult to change this complementary dance, and wondered what kept Debra and Paul stuck in such counterproductive interactions.

Structural Assessment

Structural problems in the family may also block problem-solving abilities. For example, if the mother and father in an intact family are so divided due to marital difficulties that they are unable to function as an executive subsystem, then the family will not have adequate structure to allow for effective problem solving. In addition, some structural alliances effectively block problem solving. If one parent attempts to discipline a child, and the other parent then gives privileges back to that child, the family is not developing problem-solving and parenting skills, and the child is caught in unhealthy triangles with the parents.

The key issues that the counselor must assess concern the structure of the family: the alliances between parents and children, the key triangles, and how boundaries are maintained between generations. These issues are especially pertinent when working with families.

While Ralf, a marriage and family counselor, was working with the Peterson family on some problem-solving skills, he observed that when their middle child Adam would begin acting disruptively, Mrs. Peterson would attempt to discipline him and help him act more appropriately. But while she was doing this, Mr. Peterson was winking at Adam, thereby undermining Mrs. Peterson's disciplinary efforts. Ralf's structural assessment was that structural problems stemming from marital problems were blocking problem solving and enabling the Petersons to fight with one another through their son Adam.

Cognitive Assessment

Sometimes structural or interactional interventions are adequate to produce the necessary changes in a couple or family. But at other times the couple or family has difficulty making the needed changes. For example, as Ed worked with Paul and Debra, simply understanding that they were locked in a pursuer-distancer dance was not enough to enable them to make the changes necessary for relational change to occur. The counselor may need further information to assess the underlying beliefs that help maintain the counterproductive dance. As developed by Beck (1976, 1988), cognitive therapy seeks to understand and correct the irrational beliefs that undergird counterproductive behavior.

Ellis in Ellis and Grieger (1977) popularized the theory with an A-B-C schema: A = activating event; B = belief systems; C = consequences. Many people think that an activating event (such as one person criticizing another) produces an emotional consequence (perhaps depression). But one must not leave out the belief system, which determines the meaning that a person attributes to the activating event. In cognitive therapy one's belief system, or interpretation of the activating event, produces the emotional consequences. Thus one may become depressed if one believes that a critical comment is evidence that one is totally incompetent, or that "everybody should like me and say positive things about me."

In integrative family assessment, understanding the beliefs and interpretations of events is central. For instance, Ed wondered what beliefs maintained Paul and Debra's counterproductive dance. As he continued his assessment he recognized one such belief that maintained Debra's pursuing behavior. He asked, "Debra, what would happen if for one month you did not pursue Paul in any way?" She thought for a moment and responded, "He would probably love it, and move further and further from me. In fact he probably wouldn't even think of me." She fidgeted for a few moments and then her eyes filled with tears, as she added, "He'd probably end up leaving me." For the first time Paul reached over tenderly and put his hand on her shoulder, and said, "I'm not going to leave you."

Ed realized that two beliefs were maintaining Debra's pursuing behavior. First, she believed that if she did not pursue, the relationship would get more and more distant. Thus one of her beliefs was that she was responsible for maintaining the relationship, that if she did nothing Paul would do nothing and the relationship would get worse. But beneath this belief was a related belief: if she did not keep pursuing, then she would wind up abandoned and alone.

Assessing the belief systems of two related persons usually reveals that their belief systems are complementary: the beliefs of one person reinforce the beliefs of the other. As Ed encouraged Paul to talk about what it would be like if he began to pursue more and be less passive, Paul blurted out, "If I give her an inch she will take a mile!" He added, "I'm afraid that she will never be satisfied no matter how much I try to make her happy." Paul's belief was that changing his part of the dance would be futile because Debra would only want more and more. It revealed a related belief within Paul: if he kept giving, Debra would eventually take over and he would "disappear." Diagram 2 displays the interplay of their interactions and cognitions.

Structural problems are also maintained by belief systems. Although it is frequently not difficult to assess structural problems in working with families, it is not nearly so easy to make structural changes. In counseling the Peterson family, Ralf formed a structural hypothesis about the alignment between Mr. Peterson and his son Adam. He suspected a triangle, with father and son against Mrs. Peterson, that served to deflect from a marital problem. Ralf hoped to intervene by helping the Petersons deal more directly with their marital difficulties, and then help them form a better coalition in the parenting of their son Adam. But despite all Ralf's interventions aimed at interrupting the unhealthy structure of the Peterson home, the same behavior continued. Ralf wondered what maintained their intransigence to change. He began to speculate about the belief systems that the Petersons espoused.

DIAGRAM 2
Cognition-Interaction Dance of Debra and Paul

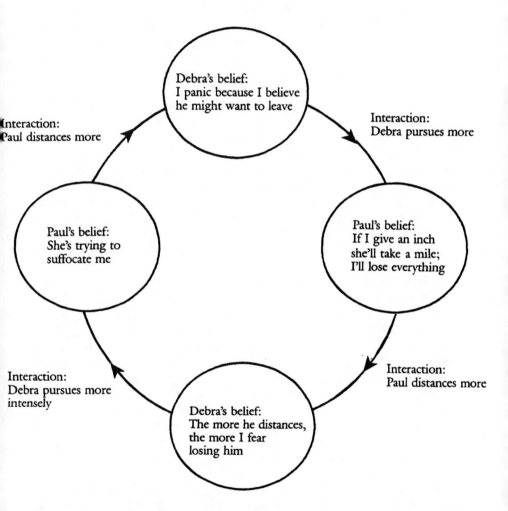

Debra's belief:
I panic because I believe
he might want to leave

Interaction:
Paul distances more

Interaction:
Debra pursues more

Paul's belief:
She's trying to
suffocate me

Paul's belief:
If I give an inch
she'll take a mile;
I'll lose everything

Interaction:
Debra pursues more
intensely

Interaction:
Paul distances more

Debra's belief:
The more he distances,
the more I fear
losing him

The cycle is complementary. The interactional dance confirms both their belief systems.

When Ralf started to explore with Mr. Peterson why he worked so stubbornly against his wife's parenting techniques, he exploded. "She tries to control everybody and everything! If I don't help Adam, she'll destroy him and make him a mama's boy." As Ralf attempted to understand this explosion, he realized that Mr. Peterson's belief about his wife's desire to control led him to fight her through his son.

Mrs. Peterson's belief was complementary. She explained calmly, "This [referring to the explosion that just occurred] is why I have to do everything. If I trust him to handle the parenting, he'll screw it up and wind up screaming at the kids. It's not worth it." Their mutually reinforcing beliefs maintained the problem and made change difficult. Ralf realized that he would have to help them not only with the structural problems but also with the belief systems that maintained their counterproductive structure.

Family-of-Origin Assessment

Belief systems frequently have their roots in family-of-origin material. For example, if one grew up in a dysfunctional family where anger erupted regularly in screaming, breaking dishes, and perhaps even physical abuse, one learned quickly that anger was bad, and to avoid it at all costs. Thus one forms a belief, frequently not verbalized and perhaps not even conscious, that anger results in destruction and therefore must be repressed. Conversely, if one grew up in a family that never expressed anger, or even other emotions, one might also believe that anger or other emotions are bad and should be repressed. One has no models to the contrary. Beliefs about anger, communication, finances, or the nature of marriage and the family usually grow out of one's childhood experience. These beliefs emerge as one creates one's own family, particularly when anxiety and stress occur.

As Debra and Paul continued their work with Ed, they gained insight into the nature of their dance, and even started to joke with each other when they noticed the dance begin. With help from Ed, they were able to clarify the belief systems that supported their dance. As Debra told Ed, however, "You know, we're both intelligent people, but it seems that these beliefs almost control us." Ed helped her think more about the power of those beliefs and reflect on her own family background, and then she was able to begin to see the origin of those beliefs. As Ed encouraged her to talk about her family, she mentioned that her father was emotionally unavailable to her, and that she tried very hard to get him to notice her. She cried softly as she talked. "I never really wanted all that much. I just wanted to know that he loved me. No matter how hard I tried and no matter how well I did, nothing changed. I kept believing that if I could just do a little better, maybe then he'd notice. I don't think he has any idea how badly he has hurt me." She sat silently for a moment, and observed, "I can't believe I'm talking about this. I always tried to pretend that it didn't bother me." Ed was able to help the couple see that Debra's beliefs about pursuing were at least partially rooted in her early experiences with her father.

Paul did not say a word while Debra was talking. Ed asked, "What are you thinking, Paul? You seem deep in thought." Paul responded, "As Debra was talking things began to click into place. I could see where Debra was coming from. But then I started thinking about my own family and found myself getting angry." Ed asked him what the anger was related to. Paul continued, "My mother was constantly on my back. She was always telling me to talk more, and always sharing her problems with me. I felt suffocated by her, and so spent as much time away from home as I possibly could." Again the room was silent. Finally, Paul laughed and said, "This is beginning to sound familiar."

Like many couples, Paul and Debra can identify the interactional patterns they are caught in, and may even recognize the belief systems underlying the problems. But assessment must frequently go to another level to help the couple or family understand and deal with the impact of previous generations, or treatment will not progress. Couples and families must be helped to see that they are the recipients of a generational legacy.

Individual Developmental Assessment

A final level of assessment is that of individual development. Although it is vital to understand the systemic functioning of a family, it is also important to remember that individuals compose family systems, and that those individuals have issues that they have brought into their families. In assessing family-of-origin issues, the counselor begins to move into this territory. But simply understanding previous generations and one's own family is not enough. The counselor must assess one final level in attempting to understand how individuals have internalized family-of-origin issues.

This assessment is largely the contribution of object relations theory and developmental psychology. Object relations theorists examine each partner's internalized representations of significant parental figures. Understanding this material is helpful in understanding the role that unconscious factors have played in mate selection, as Hendrix (1988) points out. This material is also helpful in understanding how unconscious contracts and expectations are formed between couples, as Sager (1976) and others have pointed out. Finally, developmentally informed counselors want to understand the developmental process of each marital partner: how she or he handled separation, individuation, and identity formation. The assessment procedure outlined here does not mean that individual issues will always be a focus at this level; sometimes they may be handled at the cognitive or interactional level.

In his work with Debra and Paul, Ed realized that they had not only interactional problems, which were maintained by cognitive belief systems that emerged from family-of-origin material, but also significant individual developmental issues that they needed to address. On the basis of his assessment Ed knew that Paul had had great difficulties separating from his family. As a result he tended to deal with separation issues by cutting off and distancing. Within the context of couples work, Paul would need help dealing with separation issues and defining himself to his wife. Working on individual issues is quite congruent with the Bowenian notion of differentiation of self. Bowen believed that people relate to their families of origin in a variety of ways. He developed a differentiation of self scale to reveal this; the scale shows cutoff on one extreme and enmeshment on the other. People who cut off have little emotional contact with their families of origin. People who are enmeshed are too close emotionally and cannot think for themselves. Differentiated people are able to be with their families without being emotionally reactive, and can be themselves comfortably with their families. Bowen believed that the greater the degree of differentiation of self in regard to one's family of origin, the greater the degree of marital health.

Debra had had developmental difficulties with attachment. It was clear that she had had great difficulty developing a relationship with her father, and the depth of her relationship with her mother was questionable. Because of her deep fear of abandonment, she had become a pursuer. For the marriage to move forward Debra would have to understand and resolve these issues more completely.

AN ASSESSMENT CHART

Using the integrative assessment grid, the counselor should be able to assess the couple or family on several levels. The counselor should be able to describe their problem-solving capabilities, as well as how structural and interactional problems make problem solving difficult or at times impossible. The counselor should then be able to identify and formulate a cognitive profile that spells out key belief systems and thinking styles, which in turn support problematic structures or interactional styles. These cognitive profiles or problematic belief systems most likely stem from family-of-origin material. Simply stated, as they grow up people learn to view relationships by observing how members of their families relate to each other. Part of understanding this multigenerational transmission of relational patterns is also understanding, from the framework of object relations theory, how one internalizes these early relationships and primary parental figures as one grows up. These internalizations become maps by which one unconsciously picks a mate, and at times the source of a great deal of projection and transference, as well as the basis upon which couples form unconscious contracts in terms of their expectations of each other. Transference in this context refers to the way couples unconsciously shift their feelings and unresolved issues to their spouse and try to resolve them in that context. This is different from projective identification which involves one spouse projecting unwanted or unacceptable parts of the self on the other who then collides with the projection and acts it out. Finally, by observing these transferences and projections the counselor begins to understand the individual developmental issues that each individual must resolve in the context of couples work.

A sequential assessment should give the counselor a good conceptual overview of the issues to address in couples or family therapy. Diagram 3 illustrates a completed assessment, using Paul and Debra as an example. This assessment then becomes the foundation on which the counselor builds a treatment plan. It is designed not to follow the medical model or to use the Diagnostic and Statistical Manual that lists and describes the major groups and types of psychological problems but rather to be a practical, integrative, treatment-oriented assessment model.

DIAGRAM 3
Integrative Assessment Chart for Debra and Paul

Presenting Problems	Marital troubles Communications problems Workaholism

Problem-Solving Assessment	1. State problem in concrete terms (difficulty finding quality time) 2. Talk to each other about how to solve problem

Interactional Assessment	Pursuer-distancer dance

Cognitive Assessment	Paul's belief: "If I give an inch she will take a mile" (if he gave in to Debra, Paul believed he would lose himself) Debra's belief: "If I back off Paul will leave" (if she did not pursue, Debra believed she would lose the relationship)

Family-of-Origin Assessment	Debra: father emotionally unavailable (beliefs about pursuing rooted in early experiences with father) Paul: Mother was enmeshing (beliefs about suffocating stem from early experiences with mother)

Individual Developmental Assessment	Paul: difficulty maintaining differentiation without cutting off Debra: difficulty with attachment and fears of abandonment.

4

USING AN INTEGRATIVE TREATMENT MODEL

In this integrative model, assessment provides a map that one can logically follow to form a treatment plan. This does not imply that treatment is static and simply follows an orderly outline. Rather, assessment provides a map that keeps the therapist from getting lost in the forest of treatment issues. In systemic family therapy, hypotheses are always open to revision and reformulation during integrative treatment. But treatment that is not tied to specific hypotheses and does not originate from clear assessment tends to be vague and nonspecific. Hypotheses and assessment may change as treatment proceeds, but they are a necessary starting point for treatment.

In this model, treatment may be either short-term or long-term, depending on the needs of the couple or family. At times a family is simply stuck in the midst of a developmental shift and needs brief counseling, usually of a problem-solving nature, to resolve the difficulty and move on. At other times, however, the problem is multilayered and therefore necessitates long-term treatment. Good assessment and sequential treatment planning help the counselor make that determination.

This model does not assume that treatment planning is static or unchangeable, that the counselor can set it in place at the beginning of treatment and never change it as treatment proceeds. Rather, the counselor should develop a treatment map, which starts at the simplest level (that of problem solving) and then moves sequentially through a number of treatment levels. The model understands that each couple or family is different and may therefore move through different levels of treatment. That is, one family may need to move through one or two stages of the grid, while another family may need to move through all the stages.

On the one hand, assessment is both sequential and circular. It is sequential because working on each level opens to another level. Problem solving displays interactional style, which in turn reveals belief systems that originate in both family-of-origin issues and individual developmental issues.

On the other hand, it is circular in nature. Even as the therapist goes through the assessment plan so as to get a map of issues and how they interrelate, treatment will move in a circular way. For example, once couples understand their interactions, cognitions, and family-of-origin issues, the therapist will then need to urge them to solve problems and interact in new ways. Treatment always returns to problem solving and interactions which will probably reveal additional beliefs and family-of-origin issues.

Finally, treatment planning proceeds on the assumption that treatment moves through at least three predictable stages: a beginning stage, a middle stage, and a termination stage. Each of these stages deals with several tasks and issues.

The tasks in the beginning stage include joining or engaging the family, assessing and reframing the problem(s), forming preliminary hypotheses, and setting goals for change.

While joining is an ongoing concern for marriage and family therapists, it is especially important in the beginning stage of therapy. In contrast to the work of individual psychotherapy, which requires that the therapist be constantly attuned to the individual client, in marriage and family therapy the counselor must maintain engagement with each member of the family while staying focused on the family system, not just the individuals within it. This task is not easy, because it involves conveying respect for the family and the family's view of the problem while not accepting a view that one person has the problem, which is often the way the family views the problem.

This task leads to another in the beginning stage of therapy: reframing the couple or family's view of the problem. Reframing involves moving beyond the family's suggestion that one person has the problem and attempting to put the problem in a systemic context, thus redefining it as interpersonal.

The middle stage of therapy carries out the treatment plan in the session-to-session work with the couple or family. Although some of the work of the beginning stage (e.g., joining and reframing) goes on throughout treatment, during the middle stage the focus is broader and concerned with implementing the treatment plan that was formulated on the basis of the assessment at the beginning stage.

The middle stage involves working on problem solving, continually assessing and working through interactional problems and structural problems, interpreting and helping to change couple and family belief systems, interpreting and working on family-of-origin issues, and finally understanding and working on individual developmental issues. In short-term therapy, one may not need to work on all these levels. For example, a counselor may be able to produce sufficient change in a family by working on family problem-solving skills and creating structural changes within the family without moving into the other stages. But some families or couples may have problems that require the counselor to move through many or all of the stages of this model.

The last stage of therapy is termination. In this phase the counselor reviews their progress on the goals they have selected. While initial treatment is generally once a week, if both the family and the counselor agree that they have made sufficient progress, treatment may be scaled back to once every two weeks, once a month, or even once every two months. Finally, they pick a termination date, and after again reviewing goals and progress, and making recommendations for issues that may need ongoing work, the counselor terminates treatment. The counselor may set up a follow-up appointment in two or three months to check on their progress. In one sense, termination is never final, for clients can always return to treatment if life's problems overwhelm them at any time. Rather, the counselor should remind the couple or family that problems may arise throughout life, and that if they become overwhelmed by additional problems of living, they are welcome to come back for help.

INTEGRATIVE TREATMENT

Integrative treatment begins with problem solving, just as integrative assessment did. The first step in building a treatment plan is to work with the couple or family on problem-solving skills in reference to their presenting problems. Here problem solving becomes both an assessment tool and a clear treatment focus.

As part of treatment, problem solving uses a clear set of treatment techniques. It begins by attempting to list the problems that the couple or family believes are central. The counselor then works with the couple or family to define the problem in clear, specific, behavioral terms (this step is called partializing the problem). Many clients generalize their problems in a statement like "We can't communicate," which says little about their specific problems. Their perception of the problem in such general terms may leave them feeling overwhelmed, discouraged, and hopeless. But if the counselor can help them break down their communication problem into a more specific statement, such as "we have a hard time talking about parenting without fighting," then the counselor can target specific problem-solving strategies, which, if successful, may help rekindle hope.

Some clients have difficulty even listing the problems of a marriage or family. Many family counseling sessions begin with one or both parents responding dogmatically to a counselor's question about the problem that led them to seek counseling. For example, the Martins said to Tina, their counselor, "We're here because of him!" pointing angrily at their sullen adolescent, Joe. They view their family problems as the acting out of an adolescent son, and consequently view the solution to the problem as Tina fixing Joe so he no longer acts out. Similarly, many couples begin marriage counseling by each spouse defining the problem as the other spouse. They cast the counselor in the role of the referee, who decides which spouse has the problem and needs fixing.

In either case, the role of the counselor is to reframe the problem so that the clients see it not as an individual one but as a couple or family problem or as an interactional problem. This task is easier said than done. For example, in the case of the Martin family, Tina may reframe the family definition of the problem as an interactional difficulty: the parents and the teenage son have difficulties relating. Tina would then ask them for suggestions as to what each could do to help resolve the problem. How the problem is defined and put forward is of the utmost importance. If problems are not put into an interactional frame where they can be solved, then treatment will be far more difficult.

Problem solving relies both on in-session and out-of-session tasks (Reid 1985). In-session tasks focus on what the clients can do during the session to help resolve the problem. The counselor attempts to move them away from simply talking about the problem to actively solving the problem in the room; the counselor both observes and participates in the process.

With the Martins, once the problem was defined interactionally as the three of them having difficulty getting along together without arguing, Tina encouraged them to talk together about several concrete steps each could take to help resolve the problem. As the family attempted this in-session task, Joe smugly retorted, "It's simple. Tell them to get off my back and I'll be less angry!" Tina tried to help Joe be more specific about what he meant by his parents getting off his back. Although initially frustrated, Joe eventually listed several ways that his parents could give him more space, such as not immediately pumping him for information when he came home from a party.

Not surprisingly, Tina also had to help his parents be more specific about their complaints. Their first suggestion was that Joe should just cooperate more. They too needed help to translate that request into several concrete requests for change. After both Joe and his parents listed a number of changes that they would like, Tina helped them make a contract with each other about the things they would do differently throughout the week.

This contract is an example of an out-of-session task, or homework assignment. The counselor may attempt to help the couple or family use what they have worked on in the session by turning it into an assignment that they can work on at home. The counselor must specify clearly each person's task and rehearse with the family all that could go wrong during the week. Rehearsal is important because it helps the family anticipate problems that might result from the homework. A family could become discouraged when they find that carrying out a simple assignment is much harder than they had anticipated.

Thus problem solving begins by listing the problems the couple or family brings to counseling and attempting to break down the problems into more manageable portions. Then both in-session and out-of-session tasks help the couple or family learn more appropriate problem-solving skills.

As treatment proceeds, simple problem solving is often not effective. Often the change works initially, only to result in more frustration and disappointment when it does not last. In integrative treatment, the counselor must not make the mistake of fixating on one prescription. Some well-meaning counselors keep encouraging the couple to try harder or to spend more time talking, or they attempt to come up with more ingenious homework assignments. This well-intentioned help too often leaves the family feeling even more discouraged, frustrated, and disappointed. Counselors who are more integrative in their thinking avoid this mistake by moving to another level and attempting to assess the contextual factors that block effective problem solving. In the assessment model, the two predominant contextual factors that limit problem solving are structural problems and interactional problems.

STRUCTURAL TREATMENT GOALS

When structural problems in the family hinder problem solving, the counselor's role is to have clear structural treatment goals that help the family function more effectively. The numerous structural goals all have as their aim restructuring the family. Several areas of family functioning are usually targeted: triangles and coalitions, boundaries, and hierarchies, as well as marital problems that amplify all of these issues. In targeting these areas structural family therapists assume that some types of family structures are more effective than others. Parents need to be in charge, working as partners to form an executive subsystem that effectively parents children and allows children to be children. This structure contrasts sharply with that of dysfunctional families. Children in these families often wind up parenting their parents: worrying about household finances, preparing meals on a regular basis, and living in fear about what one of their parents might do in an intoxicated state. This parentification of children illustrates dramatically the need for an effective executive subsystem that allows children the freedom to be children.

This executive subsystem necessitates a relatively healthy marriage, in which husband and wife are free to work together as partners in the parenting task and are not divided by constant marital tensions. Marital discord can lead to a variety of family problems, including triangles. For example, if a husband and wife are angry with each other but do not express it, one of the children may become the target for that anger. The diagram would look like this:

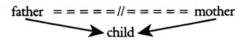

In this diagram the broken line reflects the breakdown of couple communication, and the arrows show how the parental energy gets focused on the child, resulting in the triangulation of the child.

A communication breakdown due to unresolved anger between parents results in the child receiving the parental anger and functioning as the family scapegoat. As long as the child functions in this position, usually by acting out in some way, family homeostasis is preserved. The couple does not resolve marital problems, or even examine them, as long as they make the child a scapegoat.

Another triangle forms when one of the children, usually the oldest, is cast in the role of her or his parents' marriage counselor. This child feels the awesome weight of attempting to keep the parents together, and frequently shuttles messages from one parent to the other, because the parents cannot communicate directly.

A third type of triangle is a coalition between one child and a parent against the other parent. In this triangle, the child becomes a substitute spouse and serves as a parental confidant, hearing all that parent's complaints about the other parent. This child is in an untenable position. He or she has too much inappropriate intimacy with one parent and a strained relationship with the other. The child's relationship with both parents suffers.

Many other possibilities exist for triangulation in families. The work of structural family therapy is to find ways to change these triangles. After assessing these triangles, the counselor sets treatment goals to form a more healthy structural alignment. A major goal that frequently emerges is the need to work on marital issues to enable the executive subsystem to function more effectively. This goal does not mean that marital therapy begins at that point and family therapy ends, but that counseling will focus on helping the couple be more effectual parents and find better ways of working together. It assumes that starting with parenting issues indirectly strengthens the marriage and disrupts unhealthy triangles. As improved parenting skills strengthen the marriage, the couple may choose to contract for more marital counseling to consolidate the gains they have made.

Structural goals also involve empowering parents to parent and encouraging children to be children. Although these goals sound simple, they are not accomplished by merely talking about change or assigning homework, but rather by enacting the difficult family situations in the counseling room. For example, if parents say that they cannot control their four-year-old son, the therapist waits for the child to act out in the therapy room, and then urges the parents to take charge right then and there, with the therapist serving as coach. If the parents state that they cannot agree on how to handle their son, the therapist urges them to talk to each other in the session about their disagreement.

Boundaries are of great importance to structural family counselors. Boundaries must be neither too rigid nor too flexible. If they are too rigid they prevent autonomy and create the potential for rebellion; if they are either nonexistent or too flexible they create confusion, because children do not know who is in charge. Structural family counselors aim at the creation of developmentally appropriate boundaries that allow the family to accomplish developmental tasks. At times counselors may use psychoeducational techniques, such as explaining to a family what the developmental needs for structure are within a family. At other times marital work may again be necessary to help the parents create and maintain boundaries.

A family counselor also examines generational boundaries. The counselor notes where grandparents and extended family reside; if they are close geographically and are closely involved in the family, the counselor may include the grandparents in the session. The counselor must enable parents to provide boundaries between them and their parents, so that children know who is in charge and grandparents or extended family do not undermine parental authority.

Structural family counselors might also use various techniques to intensify the session. Instead of striving for neutrality, the counselor might side with one parent to dramatize a point or to intensify the focus in a way that unbalances a family structure and makes change possible. Ironically, a counselor who attempts always to maintain neutrality and understand and interpret both persons' positions may inadvertently support homeostasis and block change. Intensification involves the therapist using several techniques to intensify an issue to help change occur, and move the issue beyond polite discussion.

In addition to in-session techniques, structural therapists use out-of-session tasks (homework) to attempt to consolidate change and to unbalance counterproductive family structures. For example, if the counselor senses that a mother is overinvolved with her ten-year-old son, who is acting out in school, the counselor may assign the father the task of doing two special things (to be negotiated in the session between father and son) with his son each week for the next four weeks. The counselor urges the mother to treat herself to regular weekly time away from the home to pursue her favorite hobby. Finally, the couple is given the task of planning a weekend away from home without their son in four weeks. With these assignments the counselor has aimed at rebalancing an over- or underresponsible marriage, and at the same time given a task aimed at revitalizing a marriage. Homework assignments are never given randomly but are always aimed at creating new structural alignments in the family.

Case Example

The Romalli family called for an appointment at the counseling center, explaining that they were worried about their nine-year-old son Tony's behavior. Tony's guidance counselor, Mrs. Roberts, had called the Romallis in for a special meeting and reported that Tony was constantly disruptive in class, seemed frequently angry, and was not turning in his homework. Mrs. Roberts explained that Tony's teacher was frustrated; all her attempts to help were failing. Mrs. Roberts reminded the Romallis that they had agreed to work with the teacher to set up a behavioral contract with Tony and that they were to reward him whenever he turned in his assignments on time and whenever he was able to get through a day without a disruption. Unfortunately the contract had failed; hence Mrs. Roberts had suggested that they try family counseling.

When Pam, a pastoral counselor, met the Romallis for the first session, she sensed immediately that they were not happy to be there. Mr. Romalli responded first to Pam's question about why they were there, saying angrily, "Because the school has had it with Tony. Now they think we have a problem." Mrs. Romalli said nothing, while Tony sat with his head down, looking quite sad, and Tony's older sister Anna looked nervous. It was obvious to Pam that Mr. Romalli intimidated the family.

Pam soon realized that problem solving was not going to work with this family. They never completed a homework assignment. Whenever they attempted to work on an issue in reference to Tony's school problem or his angry outbursts, Mr. Romalli would push his wife to take charge of disciplining Tony, while she would say little. From watching these problem-solving sequences Pam was able to formulate a structural hypothesis: She hypothesized that the Romallis' marriage was in trouble, and Mrs. Romalli was furious with Mr. Romalli's domineering methods. She felt that confronting him would be counterproductive, however, and therefore kept all her anger within. She did share some of her feelings with her son Tony, who became her confidant and seemed to carry her anger. This alliance cut Tony off from his father, with whom he desperately wanted a relationship. In this triangle everybody lost, and Pam realized that it was no wonder that Tony was acting out his anger in school.

Pam had to find ways to test her hypothesis and restructure this family to help them out of this triangle. She realized that individual counseling with Tony would not be effective because he would still be caught in a triangle, and that problem solving would not work because of the impact of the triangle. After several sessions, Pam felt that she had a good enough working relationship with them to begin pushing a little harder.

In the middle of session four, Mr. Romalli blurted out, "She never follows through with anything," looking angrily at his wife. He continued in the same angry tone to accuse his wife of not doing any of the things that the school had asked her to do. Mrs. Romalli said nothing, but her eyes filled with tears. Pam began to encourage her to respond to what her husband had said. When she did not respond, Pam interpreted: "I think you're so angry at him right now that you can't even talk. It seems like it's time for you to learn to speak when you're angry with him." Mrs. Romalli finally acknowledged that she was always angry but was afraid to express it. Mr. Romalli interrupted at that point: "If you're angry, tell me for goodness' sake!" Pam was then able to help the couple begin to deal with their anger. This was the first step of a structural treatment plan that focused on the couple learning to process their anger and gradually to rebuild their marriage.

Pam began to intensify the sessions by suggesting to Mrs. Romalli that she must not tell the children when she was angry at their father. Pam instructed Mr. Romalli to take Tony out to breakfast once a week and help him with his schoolwork. After twelve sessions, Tony's teacher reported a noticeable change in Tony's behavior.

In this case counseling interrupted a painful triangle and helped to restructure a father-son relationship. In addition, by working on some of the marital issues, Pam helped the couple form an executive subsystem that could parent more effectively. These measures did not solve all the couple's problems, but they contracted to begin working more specifically on their marriage, realizing that their deep-seated marital difficulties were causing problems for their children.

INTERACTIONAL TREATMENT PLANNING

Another likely cause of persistent difficulties with problem solving is interactional or communication problems. That interactional problems are a major cause of family pain is obvious, but what is not so obvious is that the interactional or communication solutions that families generate in an effort to solve problems can become the problem.

For example, a wife is worried because her husband has not opened up more about his feelings following the death of his mother. The more she pushes and prods him to share his feelings, the more he shuts down. This reaction only convinces her that he must share his feelings, and she tries even harder to get him to open up, but he closes down even more. In this case, the attempted solution has become the problem. More specifically, the interactional style of the couple has become a problem, leaving both parties increasingly frustrated. Their pursuer-distancer dance has increased the distance between them.

These interactional styles maintain or exacerbate the problem, at times even becoming the problem. Treatment at this level involves developing a plan to disrupt the counterproductive interactional style of the couple or family. A primary goal is to teach the couple to metacommunicate—to communicate about the way they communicate. This goal is easy to describe but difficult to accomplish therapeutically.

Most couples or families come to therapy with a fairly straightforward goal: to change their spouse, children, or parents. They have little or no self-focus. As a result a dance, or style of interaction, forms around a particular topic or goal for change, and conversation remains focused on content rather than process. The couple or family becomes so involved in the content, in both defending one's own point of view and attacking the other's, that neither can see the pattern or dance of their communication. If they can step away from the content, they can see how predictable their responses are to each other. A couple's favorite fight usually starts for the same reason, runs through the same arguments, and then ends in the same place. Rarely does anything change, and even more rarely does one spouse succeed in converting the other to her or his point of view. In the same way, another lecture by parents seldom succeeds in changing their child's study habits.

Treatment involves helping couples and families begin to clarify the patterns inherent in the way they communicate, helping them move away from content toward an understanding of process. If a couple can learn to metacommunicate and be attentive to process issues, their communication will greatly improve, and their ability to solve problems creatively should also improve.

The goal of learning to communicate about one's style of communication is not to prevent arguments or misunderstandings. It is to understand what went wrong in the process, and as one's skills become more sophisticated, to be able to recognize escalating interactions while they are happening so one can modify them before the situation gets out of control. This goal may involve a psychoeducational approach to treatment; most clients need some instruction to understand process issues, and some tools to understand what takes place in a given interaction.

One such tool is tracking. In this technique, the counselor asks the couple to reconstruct a major argument they have had recently. The counselor then helps them track their interactions in the process of the argument. They identify what sort of statements, comments, and responses intensified the interactions. With this technique couples can often quickly identify counterproductive responses that escalate interactions and block effective communication. Examples of such responses are generalizations and counterattacks, which often occur together.

For instance, a husband makes a specific criticism, such as "I did not like that dish you prepared for supper," to which his wife responds: "I knew you thought I was a lousy cook! You should have married your mother. She knows how to cook for you!" This response first moves from a specific to a general conclusion, and then follows with a powerful counterpunch. Often couples lack the communication skills and discipline needed to keep the situation under control. In this case the husband should respond: "I'm sorry that you are hurt by what I'm saying. But I'm not criticizing your cooking, I'm just saying I didn't like tonight's dinner." Unfortunately, many would respond with a counterattack, such as "Why are you always so oversensitive," or "At least my mother can cook, unlike your lazy mother!" At this point the argument is off and running and the escalation can easily get out of control.

One must have discipline and understanding to refrain from counterattacking or overgeneralizing.

Treatment helps couples do three things: identify through tracking the way interactions are blown out of proportion, begin to identify through communication skills training more appropriate responses that keep discussions on target, and learn to recognize predictable trouble spots and patterns of interaction so that they can stop the dance before it goes out of control.

Case Example

Doug and Shelly came to the first counseling session feeling discouraged and overwhelmed by the state of their marriage. They explained to Barbara, a couples counselor, in the first session that no matter how hard they tried their discussions turned into arguments, which became serious fights that then took days to work through. Both felt that the weight of the problem was the other's need to change, and hoped secretly that Barbara would realize the other had the problem and would fix that spouse. As Barbara soon found out, problem-solving attempts with this couple quickly escalated into mutual accusations. The second session began with a fight over who had done the homework correctly that Barbara had assigned. Barbara's task was to assess why problem solving was not working with this couple. She realized that their interactional style was a significant part of the problem. As a result her treatment plan began with their interactional style.

Barbara interrupted Doug and Shelly and asked them what they thought was happening in the room. Doug said sarcastically, "We're having a fight, didn't you notice?" and then laughed. Barbara pressed them to describe what was feeding the fight. After several frustrating starts she helped the couple track their interaction and see how each of them contributed to the problem: their interactional style led to rapid escalation, generalized away from the specific issue, and then resulted in attacking and counterattacking behavior. Both Doug and Shelly realized that this was their normal mode of interaction, and a key to changing their relationship.

They agreed to work on specific goals to change this interactional style. First, they would work on a list of ground rules for arguments as a way of attempting to keep things from escalating so rapidly. Barbara gave them the in-session task of talking with each other about what ground rules they thought would prevent escalation. The couple agreed to work on some specific issues, such as sticking to the subject, asking for a time-out when they began feeling frustrated, and no name-calling. As homework, Barbara asked them to talk together for one-half hour, three times a week, and during those conversations to observe any times when one or both of them was tempted to escalate the interaction. This technique aimed at teaching them to think about process, and to observe those things that might escalate future interactions.

In giving these assignments, Barbara did not assume that in themselves these techniques would produce lasting change. Rather she used them as a means of helping the couple think of process instead of content, and as a way of helping them begin to track and be aware of their interactional processes.

COGNITIVE TREATMENT PLANNING

Many couples or families know what they should be working on but find it difficult to sustain change. They frequently are not aware of the power of their belief systems to prevent change. Beck (1976, 1988), Ellis and Grieger (1977), and those in the cognitive psychotherapy field have shown the power of beliefs. Assessment often reveals that powerful belief systems can block structural change and interactional change. To be effective, counselors must find a way both to assess and to deal with these belief systems. If they are not transformed, change may not last.

Again, two techniques are best to assess and transform these belief systems: enactment and tracking. Belief systems will not simply emerge by themselves; the counselor must take an active role in helping the couple or family discern and challenge counterproductive belief systems.

The technique of enactment encourages the couple or family to talk to each other about the problem and pushes them to act out the problem in the room. As the counselor slowly intensifies the process he or she can begin to see not only structural difficulties and interactional difficulties but also cognitive problems. (The counselor must be careful not to become the family switchboard or encourage people to talk to her or him instead of to each other. If this happens enactment will not reveal the true interactional patterns or belief systems.) Particularly when the couple or family has been unable to break out of the interaction, the counselor will begin to hear some of the counterproductive belief systems emerge.

For example, as the Garcia family began to enact their controversy about their daughter Carol's refusal to go to school, the interaction between Mr. and Mrs. Garcia began to intensify. Mr. Garcia pushed angrily for Carol to attend school, and Mrs. Garcia became more concerned about the pressure he was putting on their daughter, and more reluctant to encourage Carol to attend school. Bill, the counselor, watched them escalate this interaction and wondered about the belief system that was making Mrs. Garcia stand firm in her decision. He finally said, "Mrs. Garcia, you seem convinced that your daughter should not be pushed to attend class, despite what your husband is saying. Help me understand why this is so important to you." Mrs. Garcia hesitated and then said that her husband was always putting pressure on the kids, and she was afraid that if she gave in and pushed Carol to go to school, he would just keep putting more pressure on her and she would have more problems than ever. This belief system kept her from cooperating with her husband: to exert more pressure on Carol would make her problems worse.

A second way to uncover and change counterproductive belief systems is through tracking. Tracking is used with couples to help them reconstruct arguments that occur between sessions and trace who says what, the different types of responses, and factors that lead to escalation and misunderstanding. Working with couples to track their interactions, counselors frequently find that responses seem grossly out of proportion to what was said. This disparity becomes an opportunity to explore what was heard and what belief systems it triggered.

Ted and Alice are a good example of this use of tracking. The couple came to Tom for their counseling session feeling discouraged and afraid that they were getting worse instead of better. As Tom tried to track with them what had happened to produce such a depressing week, they seemed quite confused at first. After some time they were able to isolate what had happened.

Ted had come home from a twelve-hour day at the office feeling tired and frustrated, knowing he had to go back out for one more important meeting shortly after getting home. As he walked in the door, Alice informed him that she had come home early from work feeling sick and asked if he could skip his evening meeting to stay home with her. Ted informed her that he could not do that—he had to go to the meeting. Alice muttered sarcastically, "Thanks for nothing!" For the rest of the night and for the next several days she felt depressed, while Ted was angry and frustrated. They had not been able to process what had happened and it had ruined the week. They were so discouraged by this misunderstanding that they wondered if they should even continue in counseling.

As Tom helped them track and understand their interaction, he realized that some strong belief systems must have been triggered, and he set out to identify those belief systems. He began by asking Alice what she thought about the night Ted went to the meeting. After thinking for some time, she responded, "I thought, if Ted can't come through for me in such a little thing, he would never come through for me in a major crisis. I guess I know where I stand. I'll always play second fiddle to his career."

Tom recognized two catastrophizing belief systems in her statements. First, she believed that she could generalize Ted's response to her request as clear evidence that he would not come through for her. Second, she believed that she was less important than Ted's career. These two beliefs, which Alice never bothered to talk to Ted about, left her feeling hopeless and depressed.

Ted remembered several thoughts he had that night. He thought first, "If I give in on this one, she will take advantage of me in other areas. I need to put my foot down." He also thought, "I can't believe how insensitive she is to my needs. Does she think I want to go to a meeting tonight? She has no idea how much pressure I'm under. How can I ever share my feelings with her, if she can't even tell when I'm under intense pressure?" These thoughts revealed more completely Ted's thoughts about Alice. Two beliefs that emerged were: a belief that if he gives in he will be taken advantage of, and a belief that Alice was not trying to understand him. These beliefs made him feel angry at and misunderstood by his wife. Ironically, not talking about their mutual perceptions and feelings confirmed what they believed and left them more frustrated than ever. In this case tracking helped ascertain the nature of the counterproductive belief systems.

Whether the counselor uses tracking or enactment to get at the underlying belief systems, an initial objective is to help the couple recognize and clearly articulate underlying belief systems. The next step is to help couples and families change counterproductive belief systems. This step is difficult, because these beliefs are usually well rooted as part of the way the person views the world and relationships.

A common technique for changing belief systems once they have been identified is to ask the person what the odds are that the belief is true, and then if the person can imagine any other ways of looking at the situation. Next the counselor and couple can brainstorm about other ways of seeing the situation. Using this technique, Ted and Alice saw a number of alternate ways of understanding each other's behavior and responses. They smiled sheepishly as they realized how they had jumped to conclusions about the other and turned the situation into a catastrophe.

Although it may be easy with hindsight to recognize belief systems and their effects, couples and families usually have long-standing beliefs about one another that are difficult to change. Persons can easily find evidence to confirm beliefs, such as "She really doesn't appreciate me," "His career is much more important then me," "He really doesn't like me," "If I share what I really feel I will surely get hurt," "If I get angry at him he will leave." These are a few of the beliefs that counselors commonly hear their clients describe. But they are hard to change, and the longer they are left unexamined, the more entrenched they become. Belief systems do not change simply by talking about them.

Behavioral contracting is one way to help change belief systems. It attempts to use behavioral problem-solving strategies to challenge belief systems. The counselor helps couples identify their key problematic beliefs and then specify what each partner could do to prove the other's belief wrong. This technique usually takes some degree of prodding from a counselor because couples tend to talk in generalities.

For example, when Alice said she believed that Ted would never come through for her, the counselor asked her what would convince her that her belief was not valid. Her initial response was quite general: she wanted Ted to go out of his way to be more loving. The counselor interrupted Alice to explain that one could not measure the success of such a general request. The counselor encouraged Alice to respond more tangibly and concretely. She finally said that if Ted would be home at least two nights a week by 5:30, would take her out to dinner or to a movie at least once a week, and would call to say when he was going to be home late, then she would know he was thinking of her and caring for her.

Counselors must use such concrete behavioral contracting with couples to help them change their counterproductive belief systems. It may take many such contracts to produce changes in belief systems; these beliefs will change only as they are made conscious and challenged by new experiences. If Ted did come home by 5:30, and took Alice to the movies once a week for several weeks, her old belief would be challenged by new experiences.

FAMILY-OF-ORIGIN
TREATMENT PLANNING

Dealing with belief systems, particularly those which distort couple and family interactions, frequently leads to family-of-origin issues, treatment of which is an essential part of treatment planning in an integrative model.

Many couples or families who have wrestled with attempting to change belief systems become discouraged. Attempting to change these beliefs often leads the counselor to probe the origin of these beliefs, which is usually in one's family. Although many couples may feel discouraged at this point, the fact that they have reached this point is evidence of progress. It represents tremendous growth in self-focus if instead of blaming one's spouse for one's feelings, or attempting to prove that one's spouse or a family member is the problem, the person acknowledges that he or she has some belief systems that are both problematic and difficult to change. Recognizing the problem, as well as one's contribution to the problem or at least part of it, is a large and important step.

For example, Carlos and Ramona struggled to work through some painful interactional cycles that would frequently result in Ramona shutting down and the couple not speaking to each other for weeks at a time. During their work with Sally, a marriage and family therapist, Ramona was able to isolate some of her belief systems about anger. She believed that if she expressed her anger at Carlos, a catastrophe would occur—he would probably leave her. She added that during the eleven years they had been married, Carlos had never hit her or walked out on her; he had even encouraged her to share more of what she was feeling with him. Despite several attempts at behavioral contracting, Ramona was unable to change this belief system.

As Sally explored how Ramona's family handled anger when she was growing up, Ramona began to cry. "My father was an alcoholic," she said. "When he was drinking you didn't dare do anything that might set him off. If he lost his temper someone would get hurt. I did everything in my power never to set him off." Sally went on to examine with Ramona a pattern that she had learned early in life: to keep her feelings, especially anger, locked up inside herself. She naturally transferred this pattern to her marriage with Carlos, even though she had no objective reason for doing so. Carlos sat through this discussion supportively, not understanding the power of his wife's childhood experience.

Like Ramona, many people are unaware of the power that early childhood experiences have to shape belief systems and the way one views the world. Dysfunctional families—alcoholic families, abusive families, or other types of destructive families—leave an especially powerful imprint on the psyches of their children. From these experiences one forms a set of beliefs that becomes a cognitive filter through which one views the world, and close relationships in particular. These beliefs can relate to many themes, including how to handle anger, how or whether to express emotions, how to be intimate, whether to trust people, and how vulnerable one can be.

These beliefs have the power to distort what one sees in present relationships. Thus just because Carlos encouraged Ramona to share more of her feelings with him did not mean she could do so. Her beliefs about the potential consequences of sharing feelings and expressing anger—consequences firmly rooted in her childhood experiences in an alcoholic family—made that impossible. Only when she and her counselor could thoroughly discuss and explore her childhood experiences, and when she began to understand the dynamics of an alcoholic family and the impact of living in such a family, could she gradually modify her belief systems.

In dealing with family-of-origin issues in integrative treatment, a logical starting place is the origins of specific belief systems. As with Ramona, however, this process frequently moves beyond specific beliefs and opens up many aspects of childhood experience. The counselor's main initial role is exploration, which often begins with the construction of a genogram, or family map. McGoldrick and Gersen (1985) describe the process of making a genogram, using squares for males and circles for females, and using different symbols to describe relationships between people. Constructing a map of a client's family helps the client talk more comfortably about her or his experience growing up, and helps both counselor and client see three- or four-generational patterns in the family. Clients like Ramona begin to see the multigenerational influence on their behavior.

Reading some of the books and literature on adult children of alcoholics and adult children of destructive families can help clients understand their families and provide reassurance that their feelings are normal. Through reading and through exploration of their family backgrounds clients can begin to understand the dynamics of their families in regard to parenting skills, structure or the lack of it, and family rules, in addition to what they learned about conflict, intimacy, and expectations of marriage and family. Understanding family backgrounds can be a key to help clients better understand what they have brought to their marriages in terms of conscious belief systems, which are more easily accessed and unconscious expectations that obviously are more difficult to elucidate.

Exploring their belief systems and family-of-origin material often helps couples see the types of unconscious contracts they brought into marriage and how these nonverbalized contracts may affect belief systems and communication. For example, Alice had concluded that she would never be able to count on her husband Ted, because he had refused to stay home from work to be with her when she was ill. This refusal was evidence to Alice that she could not trust Ted for a small favor, hence she could not trust him in more important matters. Exploring her belief systems led to a recognition of part of the unconscious contract that she brought into her marriage. Her father had always been distant and not a nurturing person. She had therefore resolved to marry someone more nurturing than her father, and she had thought Ted would be that type of person. But each time he failed to nurture her, Alice's hopes would be dashed and she would conclude that she could not count on him to meet her needs. In order to challenge her catastrophizing beliefs, and the depression and withdrawal that followed, she needed to understand more of the impact of her family-of-origin, as well as the way her belief systems and marital expectations grew out of her experience within her family.

As Sager (1976) and Hendrix (1988) point out, unconscious contracts are based on needs that were not met in childhood. So if a woman's father was emotionally distant, her contract in marriage might be to marry someone who will be not only emotionally present but also able to compensate for what she did not receive in childhood. Thus these unconscious contracts frequently serve a compensatory purpose: trying to make up for something that was not available in childhood.

A final goal of family-of-origin treatment is perhaps the most difficult. Multigenerational theorists like Bowen (1978) believe that change does not come simply through insight and understanding family patterns, but through making literal changes in one's family of origin resulting in a greater degree of differentiation of self. According to multigenerational theorists, this change results not from insight but by going home and changing one's response and relationships with family-of-origin members. In this stage of counseling, as persons talk about their family patterns and family structure, the counselor assesses the person's level of differentiation in relation to the family of origin. One can measure this level on a continuum between the poles of cutoff and enmeshed. Persons toward the extreme of cutoff deal with the family of origin by having as little contact as possible, by staying distant. In effect they have not dealt with family of origin at all, but have simply stayed as distant as possible. They are not confident that they can maintain differentiation if they spend too much time with their families, and feel as if they are fifteen again after spending three days with their families. On the other extreme, those who are enmeshed with their family of origin frequently live close to their family and do not make independent decisions without consulting their mother and father. This situation can be a source of great frustration to their spouse, who wishes that they would be more independent.

Whether one is enmeshed or cut off, the goal is to become more differentiated in regard to one's family of origin. Differentiation does not mean being hostile to one's family of origin, angrily informing the family of all the ways they have hurt one in the past. Rather it means learning to be oneself in regard to one's family of origin, and not getting hooked into the same old interactional battles and games that happen so predictably. Differentiation frees energy to work more creatively on one's marital or family problems.

Bob and Joann are an example of this problem. When they began counseling they were locked in a pursuer-distancer dance: Joann pursued and Bob distanced. In addition they fought over the fact that Bob spent little time with their children. In their work with Harold, they made some progress in breaking that predictable pattern of interaction. In so doing they were able to recognize some disruptive belief systems and make changes in them. As they explored the way their belief systems had formed in their families, however, it became evident that Bob had cut off from his family of origin and was in danger of emotionally cutting off from his present family. When he began to recognize this pattern it frightened him, and he told Harold that he desperately wanted to change the pattern. Harold suggested that Bob find a way to build a relationship with his own father, from whom he had emotionally cut off years ago. At this point Harold served as a coach to help Bob reconnect with his father. Harold focused on ways of helping Bob maintain nonanxious presence with his father and focus on changing himself and his own reactions, as opposed to attempting to change his father. By rebuilding a relationship with his father, Bob was able to reconnect with his wife and slowly begin to connect with his children in a new way. This is gradual, long-term work that requires commitment on the part of couples and families. But in order for change to last, one must make change at this level of generational issues.

INDIVIDUAL DEVELOPMENTAL ISSUES

A final level of treatment, perhaps the most difficult to do in the context of marriage and family therapy, is to work on individual developmental issues. In working with family-of-origin issues, counselors sometimes begin to see deeper underlying issues that must be resolved in order for couple or family issues to progress. Four common issues are projective identification, splitting, unresolved grief, and childhood abuse (physical, sexual, or emotional).

Projective identification occurs when one projects unwanted or unacceptable parts of the self onto someone else in the family and then attacks those parts in that person. For example, a man who is out of touch with his feelings is likely to marry someone who is very emotional. The husband then projects his feelings onto his wife, who becomes the container for his feelings—she ends up doing all the emotional work for both of them. This relationship is called collusion. The therapist's task is to help clients recognize their projective identifications and then learn to withdraw them.

Parents can also project onto their children and then attack them. If a father has not worked through his unresolved sexual feelings, he may project these feelings onto his teenage daughter. He may become overly protective and restrictive, carefully monitoring her activities and dating life and perhaps accusing her of being sexually active and then grounding her unfairly.

Projective identification has many variations. One variation of parental projection frequently occurs after a divorce. The custodial parent unconsciously associates one of the children with the ex-spouse and projects the ambivalence and anger felt toward that spouse onto the child. That child often becomes the scapegoat; the parent views the child as having problems similar to those of the former spouse. Thus if a wife saw her ex-husband as angry and hostile, she will see the child as angry and hostile. The parent then unconsciously attempts to change the negative traits in that child that she or he could not change in the former spouse. Again, the treatment goal at this level is to help clients recognize their projections, which tend to be unconscious, and then help them withdraw those projections from the child and see the child in a more realistic way.

Projective identification can be a major problem in both parenting issues and marital issues. Unless these projections can be recognized and withdrawn, problems will probably continue, no matter how well couples and families learn communication skills or problem-solving techniques. The counselor may at times work nondirectively, allowing the client to begin to see the projections; at other times the counselor may be quite direct in offering interpretations.

In working with the Lee family, Susan became aware that Mr. Lee was easily irritated by his thirteen-year-old son. Although the family had done some good work in their family therapy, the interactions between Mr. Lee and his son had rapidly escalated. Both Mr. and Mrs. Lee recognized what was happening, and both understood that Mr. Lee and his father had had a high-pressure relationship. But Mr. Lee's relationship with his son did not change until Mr. Lee was able to recognize his own lack of ambition, and the fact that he had never really been successful. These feelings were deeply painful to him, and he had a great deal of difficulty even talking about them in the session. But when he identified his own feelings, he was then able to recognize, to his chagrin, that he was most frustrated with his son about the

same issues that he felt bad about within himself. Understanding this projection gave Mr. Lee some clues for the first time about why his relationship
with his son was so intense.

Splitting is a rather primitive defense, originating from problems in the
first few years of life. Persons who employ splitting as a defense mechanism
tend to see people, issues, situations, and so forth as either all bad or all good,
as black or white with no shades of gray. Thus they are uncomfortable with
ambivalence. If they are hurt by someone they love, they can easily conclude
that the person is now all bad and therefore not to be trusted. They have
difficulty accepting the fact that the person they love has both good and bad
qualities. Because they cannot tolerate this tension, which is a necessary part
of all human relationships, they must conclude that their spouse is either all
good or all bad.

Splitting makes couple or family work very difficult. The counselor must
help the client deal with the tendency toward splitting and become more
tolerant of ambivalence. This work is slow and difficult, and the counselor
may not be able to do it in the context of couples or family work. In this
case the counselor may refer the person for individual psychotherapy to work
on resolving some of these issues, while continuing the couple or family
therapy. Or the counselor may seek to integrate some individually focused
work as part of the couple's work, with the spouse observing and supporting
the treatment. In so doing, the counselor must be careful not to imply that
one person has the problem, but simply that for now one person needs more
of the focus, and later in treatment the other may need more of the focus.

When Joyce first began couples therapy with her husband Alan, they
worked on several important marital issues. Their attempts at problem solving
did not work well, and soon revealed a painful pursuer-distancer dance. They
tracked this dance through several strongly held belief systems, which were
difficult to disrupt and which were rooted in their experiences in their own
families of origin. When Alan did not respond to Joyce's initiatives, she became
enraged, screaming at Alan that he did not love her. Alan became increasingly
discouraged and felt that no matter what he tried, he always failed. Therapeutic
attempts to deal with this painful interaction were invariably unsuccessful.

Christine, their counselor, realized that couples therapy alone was not going
to resolve the problem. After working for a while to help Alan develop coping
strategies to deal with Joyce's rage, Christine suggested that Joyce begin to
work on her own issues. It had become clear in their work together that
Joyce had suffered from the emotional abuse of neglect in her family of origin.
As she began to work on these issues, powerful feelings of loss began to
emerge, leaving her shaken for hours after some sessions. For the first time
in her life she began to realize how neglected she had been as a child. Because
both her parents were alcoholics, she had had to be responsible for everything.
When Christine asked gently who had nurtured her as a child, Joyce could

think of no one, and she felt overwhelmed by that realization. As she continued to work on these issues, she realized the magnitude of the pain she had internalized over the course of her life, and how she had transferred much of the blame for that pain to Alan. In this case, without that realization marital counseling would never succeed.

Like Joyce, many clients must look at old childhood issues before being able to move forward with couples or family therapy. Unresolved grief issues or unresolved childhood abuse issues often cause problems in current relationships. Unless one can go back and work at understanding and resolving those old hurts—obviously a difficult process—current relationships may suffer. Whether this work can be done in the context of marital therapy or needs to be referred to another therapist is debatable, with much support for both sides. But doing some of this individual work in the presence of the spouse, who thereby gains a more empathic understanding of his or her spouse and can be more supportive, seems preferable.

A TREATMENT PLANNING GRID

Like integrative assessment, integrative treatment planning follows a grid that begins with problem solving, and moves through stages of interactional treatment, structural treatment, cognitive therapy, family-of-origin therapy, and finally individual developmental issues. Treatment need not cover all these stages. The family determines the extent and nature of treatment. For some families, work at the problem-solving and structural levels may be sufficient, and treatment terminated. Other families may need to go further.

Therapy moves through the stages in a circular, not a linear, fashion. For example, as couples are able to isolate specific problematic belief systems, they will move back to problem-solving skills as a way of changing the beliefs. As they work on family-of-origin material, they will in turn move backward through the grid and see how their beliefs were formed in childhood, and then return to problem-solving skills to look for ways to change the beliefs, or even make changes within families. Thus while assessment is more sequential in trying to formulate a basic map, treatment is more circular. It moves through various stages but always back to problem solving and improved communication.

At the conclusion of treatment, the couple or family should have increased knowledge of their interactional style, their structure, their cognitive beliefs, and if they continue long enough, more awareness of their family-of-origin material. Growth in these areas should result in a greater ability to do their own problem solving with increased creativity, so that they can manage the normal developmental difficulties of life. Diagram 4 summarizes treatment planning and techniques at each level.

DIAGRAM 4
Treatment Planning

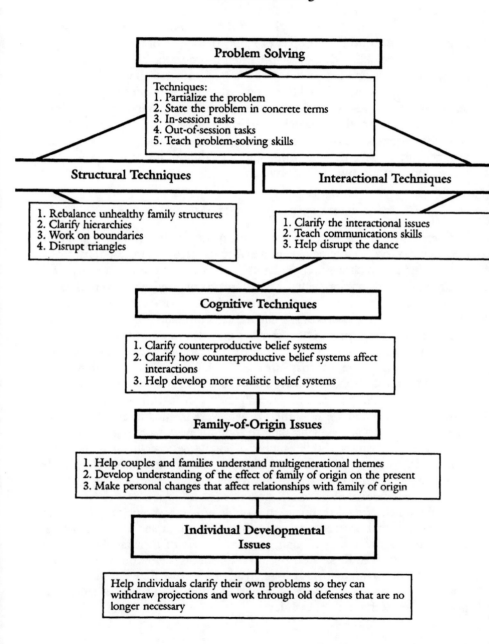

5

APPLYING THE
INTEGRATIVE MODEL

The integrative model is designed for use with a wide variety of couples and families: those needing long-term or short-term therapy, those at one of the many developmental transitions, and those with a vast array of problems.

Three case studies demonstrate the model's range of application. First, the case of the Joneses illustrates a family in need of short-term family counseling. Second, the Humfelts represent a case needing longer treatment (35 sessions) to cover different types of issues. Finally, the Packers are an example of a couple needing long-term couples work, in this case almost three years. All three cases are summarized in terms of the process of therapy and in terms of the specific techniques used as a way of illustrating the application of the integrative model. Treatment grids for each of the cases illustrate the flow of treatment and summarize the specific techniques and interventions used.

CASE STUDY 1: THE JONES FAMILY

The Jones family, consisting of Steve and Linda and their three children, Tim (age 13), Jane (11), and Tonya (10), came reluctantly for their first family therapy session with Julia. The school system had referred them because Tim's teacher, Mrs. Gordon, said he was having problems in school—not turning in homework assignments and disrupting the class. Mrs. Gordon wondered if he might be depressed, and suggested family counseling, warning the family that Tim was in danger of repeating the grade.

Julia, the family counselor, welcomed the family into her office. She noticed immediately that they seemed tense about being there. After trying to join with them and make them comfortable by talking about the latest snowstorm, she asked if each member of the family would state in his or her own words why they were there for counseling. No one responded.

Finally, Steve broke the silence. "I guess I should start," he said slowly. "I can't believe that we're here. The school said we should get some family counseling because Tim might stay back. I have no idea what's gotten into him." Linda added, "He's never been like this before; we have no idea why he's having so much trouble." Tim sat sadly through their conversation, and said nothing at all. Both of his sisters were confused about why they were there. Tonya summed up their confusion bluntly: "If Tim is the problem why are we here? He's the one in trouble." Linda broke in quickly and asked Julia, "Do you think you can help Tim?"

These themes frequently emerge in the first session of family therapy. The rest of the family often sees the child who manifests a problem as the identified patient, and as a result they are not sure why they are even there. The initial task of the counselor is to join adequately with the family and then help build a frame that enables the family to understand why they should all continue in family therapy and make sure they return for the second session. Julia accomplished this goal by explaining that her job was much easier to do with the help of the entire family. She was careful not to challenge the family's frame too much in the first session, but told them she could sense that the problem with Tim was becoming a problem for the whole family, and that as a family who cared about each other they could probably find a way to help each other. By highlighting the family's strength she was able to join more effectively with the family.

In addition, Julia realized that she was dealing with yet another system: the school system. At the end of the first session she asked the family to sign a release of information form so Julia could talk with the school system to get another perspective on the problem. Families are involved in a variety of systems, of which the school system is a very important one. Connecting with the school system and getting more information on how Tim interacted with peers and with teachers as well as any additional information could be very helpful in the counseling process.

In the first two sessions Julia struggled to develop a hypothesis to explain why Tim was suddenly having so much trouble in school after years of solid academic performance. As she encouraged the family to talk about the past year, important information emerged. Although Tim continued to sit quietly, Tonya said: "It's been a tough year. We had to move to this dumb state, and leave all our friends in New Jersey, and go to a new school." Jane broke in: "Well, I really like my new school and new friends. I don't know why you don't like it here." Tonya countered, "I miss my friends and my house."

This was the first that Julia had heard about a move. She asked, "How about you Tim, what was the move like for you?" Tim glared at her for a moment, then said, "I finally got on a good soccer team, and right in the middle of the season we had to move. The team in this school stinks, and anyway I got here too late to try out for it."

Linda's eyes filled up with tears as she listened to her children talk about the move. "It's been hard on all of us," she said softly. "We had no idea how stressful this move was going to be, or how rooted we had been in our old community."

Steve began to look uncomfortable. "I feel so guilty about all this. The move was important for my career; if I had turned it down, I couldn't advance in this corporation. I didn't feel that I had much choice."

Linda came quickly to his defense. "He really didn't have much choice. Steve always tries to do what's best for the family, and this was something he felt he had to do. I supported his decision."

Julia began to feel more optimistic as she saw a way to reframe the family's problem away from Tim's difficulties in school. She tried to summarize what she was hearing in a way that would help reframe the problem for the family. "It seems that as a family you have gone through a major transition this year." "That's an understatement," Linda muttered. Julia continued, "Obviously the move has affected each of you differently. But as a family the change has been major. Can you talk more about how you, as a family, have handled the move?"

As the family talked further about the impact of the past year, it became obvious to Julia that they had previously talked little about it. Steve had felt pressured into taking the transfer and had not talked much about how it was going to affect the family, even though he felt guilty about the possible repercussions on his family's well-being. Linda had grown up in the part of New Jersey they had moved from and had a strong network of friends and family in that area. In addition she had just begun a new job, after having stayed home with her children while they were small. She obviously had not wanted to move, but she felt she had to support Steve because she knew how hard it was for him. She had decided that the best thing she could do would be to support Steve as much as possible and keep her own feelings to herself. Thus she and Steve had not communicated much, and Julia began to wonder if Linda was angry with Steve but determined not to let it out.

So many of their feelings had been locked up that the family had hardly been able to talk about the transition. Much of this emotional blockage was related to the difficulty Steve and Linda had had in discussing more honestly their feelings about the move and the implications of the move. With this assessment information, Julia could formulate her hypothesis and begin to work at the first level of the treatment grid: problem solving.

If part of the problem was the family's difficulty with a major move, then one of the problem-solving skills needed was the ability to talk more freely and directly about the transition. Julia believed that talking more openly might indirectly help some of Tim's school problems.

Tim in particular seemed relieved to find that others in the family were also experiencing difficulty with the move and that he was not alone in his feelings. "I thought that I was the only one who didn't like it here." He was surprised that his mother was finding it hard to adjust to the new area and still had not found new friends. This was the first time he had heard his mother talk openly and honestly since they had made the move. He was also surprised to hear his father talk about how guilty he felt for moving the family in order to accommodate his career objectives.

After the third session the family was noticeably encouraged, and Julia felt that treatment was going well. They had begun talking more regularly, had been able to do more creative problem solving at home, and had planned several outings since they started therapy.

At the fourth session, Julia was caught off guard when Linda began by saying, "These sessions have been helpful, but Tim is still in danger of failing. What do we do about that? That is why we came in the first place." This sort of occurrence is common in family treatment. Although the family initially goes along with an interactional way of looking at the problem, sooner or later they return to the presenting problem if it has not cleared up.

At first Julia felt defensive, but she realized that the family must be frightened. Instead of responding defensively, or reminding the family of the progress they had made, she joined with them and complimented the family on their concern for Tim. As she reviewed with the family the strategies they used to help Tim, she again realized how depleted the family was, and she perceived that Steve was largely outside the family.

When she asked more about Steve's role in the family, she found that he had been so involved in his new position that he frequently worked twelve- to fourteen-hour days and was largely unaware of what was happening in the family, particularly of the problems Tim was having. Linda did not want to push Steve, even though she was frustrated and overwhelmed by the problems, because she did not think that he could tolerate any more pressure. As a result the family was like a pressure cooker, with everyone feeling overwhelmed.

Julia realized that a second phase of treatment needed to begin. Contextual factors were blocking resolution of the presenting problem despite increased problem-solving skills. Therefore interventions were needed to deal with some of the structural issues in the family: Julia needed to help empower the parents to deal more effectively with the family's problems in general, and Tim's problems in particular. In this second phase Julia's primary goal was to rebalance the marital system by enabling Steve to take more of a parental position within the family.

Her first intervention was to invite only the parents to come in for two sessions; she knew that the couple would be reticent to discuss marital issues in front of the children. Steve and Linda reluctantly agreed to come, if Julia really felt that these sessions would help Tim and his school problems. Julia assured them that the sessions would help Tim; she did not want to raise undue anxiety in the couple by implying that the problem was in the marriage. Like many couples, they might be offended by that assumption and drop out of therapy prematurely. It is wise to help couples see that their marital work is always in the interests of the children.

Steve and Linda arrived for the session noticeably more nervous than in previous sessions. The session started slowly. Julia reviewed with them all their attempts to help Tim with his school problems. It became clear to Julia that Linda was doing all the work with Tim. When Julia inquired about this situation, Linda became defensive and said, "What do you expect? Steve works late every night, and I don't want to put any more pressure on him. How much more can he take?" "What do you think, Steve?" Julia asked. Steve thought for a moment, then said sadly, "I have felt so out of it in terms of the kids' lives. I think I can't afford not to have more input into their lives."

As Julia explored with them what they could do differently, she realized that Linda had been protecting Steve from a great deal of her anger. This anger began to emerge slowly, with gentle prodding from Julia. The anger did not surprise Steve; he said he had felt Linda becoming progressively more distant. "Why didn't you ask me about it?" Linda said, beginning to cry. "I have felt so overwhelmed, and desperately needed you." Steve was initially uncomfortable, but Julia helped him listen empathically to his wife's feelings. Julia thought it was important for the couple to work through these feelings because she hypothesized that Tim had become the container for Linda's unexpressed anger. Only as Linda and Steve could talk about the anger would Tim be freed from carrying it. Julia encouraged the couple to talk more to each other about their feelings; they were hesitant at first but then began to make substantial progress in opening up to each other both in the sessions and at home.

Linda began the next session by saying, "We used to be able to talk about anything, including anger and irritation. But since this move, it seems as if everything shut down. It's almost like this move took so much energy that we had nothing left for each other. It feels good to be talking again." Steve nodded his agreement and squeezed his wife's hand. Julia attempted to provide a frame for what had happened. She explained that sometimes stresses can build to such a point that couples and families can temporarily exhaust their resources. Couples who have had a strong marriage based on a history of good communication skills can recover much more easily. Both Steve and Linda seemed relieved by that explanation.

Now that they were talking again, and some of the tension between them was resolved, Julia could help them begin to work with Tim on his school problem. Addressing this problem earlier would most likely not have succeeded, because the structure of the family system needed to shift in order to accommodate change. To avoid repeating old mistakes, Julia began by reviewing with them their previous attempts to help Tim. With Julia's help they came up with a plan. Steve would work out a system with Tim, whereby he would bring home assignment sheets on a regular basis that the teacher would initial when they were done. If Tim were able to do the assignments for a week, he and his father would do something special together that weekend. Julia encouraged Linda to do something positive for herself; she both deserved and needed a break. Finally, Julia asked the couple to make a commitment to go out alone at least once a month, something they had rarely done since the move.

Although these appeared to be simple problem-solving behavioral interventions, they were in fact attempts to shift the family's structure, which had become dysfunctional due to the effects of the move and all that was associated with it. The first structural need was to rebalance the marital system by helping the couple work through the distance and anger between them. Only in working through this material could the couple function more effectively as parents. A second structural move involved helping Steve reenter the family. The stress of his career had temporarily moved him out of the family and put all the parental pressure on Linda. If step one was to help he and Linda talk about that transition and work through their feelings about it, then step two was to involve Steve directly with Tim and make him responsible for carrying out a solution. Step three was helping Linda give up some of her responsibility and begin doing some things for herself, to lessen the threat of enmeshment in Tim's problem. The final step was to help the couple nurture and build their marital relationship by going out more, thereby keeping them functioning better as parents.

After eight sessions Julia agreed with the family that they had met their goals. Tim's teacher noticed a slow but steady improvement, but more importantly the family was better able to talk to each other and once again to handle their problems on their own. They agreed to come back in a month to see if they were continuing to make progress: "sort of a checkup," as Tim put it.

Treatment does not always go as well and end on such a positive note after only eight sessions. It is important to note that this family had a good foundation; their problems were due largely to their responses to great stress. By using their strengths, Julia was able to help them make rapid progress.

This case study displays the application of the model to families who are in transition, or who are stuck and who can be helped with short-term therapy. In this case therapy moved through only the first two stages: the problem-solving stage and the structural stage (diagram 5). Treatment could end after stage two, because this family had a solid foundation from which to work.

CASE STUDY 2: THE HUMFELTS

On the advice of their pastor, George and Diana Humfelt came to see Sarah, a marriage and family counselor, for their first session. Their presenting

DIAGRAM 5
The Joneses

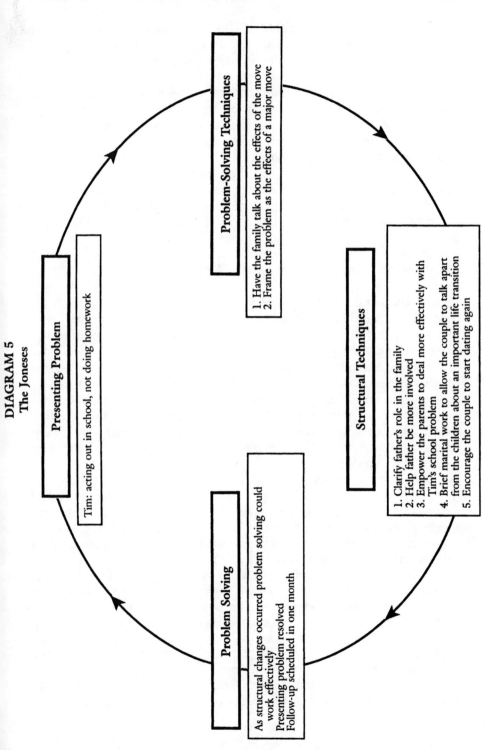

Presenting Problem

Tim: acting out in school, not doing homework

Problem-Solving Techniques

1. Have the family talk about the effects of the move
2. Frame the problem as the effects of a major move

Structural Techniques

1. Clarify father's role in the family
2. Help father be more involved
3. Empower the parents to deal more effectively with Tim's school problem
4. Brief marital work to allow the couple to talk apart from the children about an important life transition
5. Encourage the couple to start dating again

Problem Solving

As structural changes occurred problem solving could work effectively
Presenting problem resolved
Follow-up scheduled in one month

problem was that they had difficulty talking to each other. Most of their discussions turned into arguments, which ended with George shutting down and withdrawing, while Diana became more frustrated. They also said that many of their arguments revolved around money. More specifically, as Diana pointed out, the arguments were about not having enough money. George sat silently during Diana's description of their problems. He finally added, "That's a matter of opinion. Diana never believes there's enough money. I admit I would like there to be more of it, but we get by."

Sarah encouraged George to describe why he thought they had come for counseling. He replied with a somewhat patronizing air, "Diana is never happy. It's always something. It's either that we don't have enough money, or I'm not meeting her needs, or I'm not home enough. I really believe that Diana needs to discover what's missing within her so that she can find happiness. I will never be able to meet all her needs." Diana retorted, "I'm hardly talking about you making me happy. I'm just looking for us to be able to talk about things that are uncomfortable. You're so afraid of any tension or emotion."

Sarah realized that she needed to intervene and help the couple frame the problem in terms that would enable them to begin working together on it. She summarized their interaction by saying, "It's obvious that both of you are really frustrated right now by what the other is saying. Is this indicative of the way things usually go between you?" Both Diana and George assured her that things usually got a lot worse. Sarah went on to explain that every couple has an interactional dance, which they predictably do around specific problems, that keeps them stuck. She explained that in meeting weekly, they would attempt not only to work on their presenting problems but also to clarify and improve their communication skills. Thus she attempted to provide a frame from which to do therapy.

Phase one involved helping this couple clarify the problems that brought them into treatment and beginning to evaluate their dance as they attempted to solve those problems. For the second session they prepared a list of problems they had formulated during the week. They both listed disagreements about money as a problem. A major problem for George was that Diana never seemed happy. Diana retorted that a major problem for her was that George was never emotionally available: "he seems to check out emotionally." They both agreed that in-laws were a problem, specifically that George's family was a problem for Diana (George enjoyed being with Diana's family). They also mentioned that George, a CPA, worked for his father's accounting firm. Diana quickly added, "That's why we never have enough money." Both agreed that relations with George's family were difficult, and that they would need to address that issue at some point in therapy.

As George and Diana worked with Sarah on these presenting problems, they acted out their dance in the room, with Diana pursuing and George becoming quieter and distancing in his own way. This dance kept them from being able to resolve those problems; Sarah knew that problem-solving techniques were not going to succeed with this couple. Their interactional patterns kept both of them frustrated and disappointed.

As is often the case, each felt that the problem was with the other and came hoping that therapy would change the other. George was convinced that if only Diana had some insight into her own problems, and perhaps some individual psychotherapy to help her be more self-reliant, then she would not be so needy, and he would be able to enjoy being with her more easily. Diana was equally convinced that if only George would spend more time with her, and not back away from conflict and unpleasant subjects, then she would not always pursue him. She insisted that she was sick of being the pursuer, the one who always needed to take charge in their relationship. Both looked to Sarah to be the referee and decide who had the problem. On some level each hoped to be vindicated, and the blame assigned to the other. Neither had much awareness of her or his contribution to the problem.

Sarah decided to move to level two of the model and began to focus on their dance as the target for change. She worked with them to help them understand the predictability of their dance and began to push them to recognize it as it was happening. She used two basic techniques. First, she spent a significant amount of time tracking with them. For example, George and Diana began the fourth session by stating that they had had a terrible week, which began with a disagreement over purchasing a new washing machine. Diana felt that the problem was that she could not get George to talk with her about their need for a new washing machine, and whether they could afford one. George stated that Diana always picked the worst time to raise such issues, and that once she began to get upset, he refused to talk further. Each blamed the other.

Sarah helped them explore the sequence of the interaction and track it one piece at a time. She asked them to reconstruct how it had started. Diana began by saying, "It started innocently enough. All I said was we need to decide what to do about the washing machine." Sarah inquired what happened next. George stated that he said very little, because he was watching the news on television. "As always, Diana had to push harder because I didn't respond the way she wanted me to," he added. From there Sarah tracked carefully with the couple how the interaction escalated until they were both frustrated and angry. Both agreed that Sarah had a good sense of how the argument proceeded and escalated. Both claimed that this argument was also representative of their interactions.

Sarah then asked them to go back over the interactional loop and talk about what each of them could have done differently. She helped them look at alternative ways they could have responded. For example, Diana could have acknowledged that George was watching the news and asked him when would be a good time to talk about the washing machine. George could have explained to Diana that he wanted to finish watching the news, but would like to talk about the washing machine later in the evening. Going through this exercise with Sarah helped the couple see two things: the interactional feedback loop that they create, and what each of them could have done to break the cycle.

With these issues the goals of therapy are to reduce blaming, increase understanding of the interactional feedback loop, and increase self-focus. One hopes that clarifying the interactional feedback loop helps the couple recognize the dance as it is happening and learn new communication skills that will help them alter counterproductive interactions. The basic techniques used at this stage are tracking misunderstandings that have happened during the week, enacting some problems during the session to clarify the interactional feedback loop, and then teaching some new communication skills, such as active listening and conflict resolution. The couple cannot learn these skills if they continue the escalation by blaming each other. The counselor must help both partners understand that problems in couples communication result from unproductive communication sequences in which both partners participate. The goal of therapy is not to change the individual but to change the interaction. When couples can accept this premise, change can occur.

After several weeks of working in this manner some changes had occurred for the couple, and they reported a greater ease in their communication. But both were still frustrated. George summed up the struggle: "I understand what I need to do, but somehow I keep getting stuck." Diana nodded her agreement. Sarah realized that they must move to a deeper level to consolidate the gains and accomplish more growth. At the cognitive level they could attempt to understand the belief systems through which each interpreted the interactions of the other. They had already begun to work on this level; both George and Diana often attempted to explain why they did the things they did. But Sarah needed to work more explicitly at this level.

Moving in this direction with this couple involved using the same techniques of enactment and tracking as a way of further examining the interactional sequences, but looking below the interaction for the way in which belief systems might distort communication. Two powerful beliefs were beginning to emerge with this couple. Diana knew from their work thus far that she should not pursue George so much. George knew that he should attempt to listen better and not back away when Diana raised issues. Yet both remained caught in the counterproductive cycle unaware of the power of their belief systems.

Sarah asked Diana what she was afraid would happen if she stopped pursuing George and stopped being overresponsible. Diana seemed puzzled at first. Then she said, "I think I'm afraid that if I did not take the initiative to talk about unpleasant subjects, George would never bring them up and they would never get talked about at all." "What would happen from there?" Sarah asked. "I think we'd just get further and further apart and finally George would leave," Diana said, as her eyes filled with tears. George seemed surprised by what Diana was saying and tried to reassure her. Sarah helped Diana clarify her beliefs about pursuing, realize how powerful these beliefs were, and see how they made it difficult to stop pursuing.

George also needed to understand what was behind his reluctance to initiate discussions and talk about potentially tense subjects. As he worked at understanding what he believed about Diana, he realized that he believed that she could not keep anything on small levels, that she would inevitably escalate matters. Thus for George to bring up a subject meant to risk that subject escalating and becoming unpleasant. As a result he avoided subjects that might cause problems. George also realized that he generalized this belief about Diana to apply to women in general, hence it was best never to have a controversial discussion with a woman. After he said that, he looked embarrassed. "I can't believe I really believe that, yet it is certainly consistent with the way I act."

Sarah was able to help the couple understand the complementarity of their beliefs—the beliefs of each reinforced the beliefs of the other—and how their belief systems blocked communication. As George withdrew from controversial discussions with Diana, she would pursue him with more frustration. When they would finally have the discussion, Diana's frustration would come through. This reaction would confirm George's beliefs: women were always too emotional. He then backed away, confirming Diana's fear that if she did not pursue, nothing would happen between them.

Once they recognize the belief systems, some couples are empowered to change the interactional patterns and solve problems effectively. Other couples, like Diana and George, can frequently recognize these dysfunctional belief systems, but attempts to change them are discouraging. As a result, couples therapy often moves quickly into family-of-origin issues after these beliefs are clarified.

This was true for Diana and George. As they continued to work on their belief systems and communication patterns, they became aware of how powerful those beliefs were. Yet they were confused because the beliefs seemed irrational; they adhered to them even though they had little or no evidence to support these beliefs. This realization led to discussion of family-of-origin material.

Sarah asked George if he had ever had similar feelings before and felt pressured to withdraw from difficult interactions. George smiled and said, "I always felt that way growing up. I did whatever I could to stay clear of all the conflict." Having done a genogram for both George and Diana at the beginning of counseling, Sarah remembered that George was the oldest of three children and that he had described his family as marked by conflict.

She encouraged George to describe more of the conflict and how it started, but he found it difficult to specify the nature of the conflict.

Instead, George talked about his father, whom he described as a workaholic; he had worked many eighty-hour weeks to build up his accounting firm, which now was the largest in the area. He added that his father was domineering and explosive, especially after he had been drinking. When Sarah asked him more about this drinking, he said that his father would drink episodically as a way of alleviating stress. But after several drinks he would become more explosive than usual. "At that point everybody would head for cover, because there was no reasoning with him once he had crossed the line," George said.

He then mentioned that his mother would begin drinking every day as she prepared dinner, and would always have two drinks with her meal. When Sarah asked what happened after dinner, George began to get tense. Diana jumped in. "I've always thought George's parents were alcoholics, but whenever I mention that George gets very angry." George was getting more uncomfortable by the minute. Sarah gently encouraged him to go on. George proceeded reluctantly to describe how his mother would continue to drink wine after dinner; by eight thirty every night she would doze off on the couch.

Sarah said carefully, "Many people think that all alcoholics are on skid row, and so an upper-middle-class family, whose father has never missed a day of work, and where all the physical needs are met, could not be alcoholic. But any household in which alcohol occupies a central place—like yours—is alcoholic." Sarah provided some education about alcoholism to help George and Diana understand its effects on a family. By this point George was emotionally shaken. "I've never looked at it the way you've just described. I have a lot of thinking to do." He was quite relieved that the session was over.

In future sessions George was able to identify a four-generational pattern of alcoholism in his family, and was beginning to see what a powerful force it had been when he was growing up. Sarah had encouraged George to read some books on adult children of alcoholics, which also prompted some powerful emotional reactions in him. He identified with much that he read, and was both frightened by what he was seeing in his family and relieved that his feelings were normal.

Gradually things were making sense to George and to Diana. At one session George looked tearfully at Diana and said, "You wonder why I don't like tension or conflict? When my parents were drinking conflict might lead to all kinds of craziness. I was afraid that somebody might get killed. I spent my whole childhood trying either to make peace and make sure that everything was running smoothly, or to run for cover. Now I'm supposed to see that conflict might bring intimacy! Can you see what a contradiction that is for me?" Diana nodded knowingly. Together they were understanding more about the source of George's interactional style and beliefs. But they needed to do more work.

One significant problem that continued was the issue of money. George still worked for his father and was underpaid even though he put in long hours. Sarah knew that change must occur not only in one's head, in the form of insight, but also in behavior, in action. George's work-related issues with his father were a good place to begin, and George was now eager to try. Sarah became more of a coach as they began to plan for him to stand up to his father assertively but nonaggressively for the first time in his life. The confrontation went well; although George did not get the raise he wanted, he did gain confidence in realizing that he could stand up to his father. He resolved that if in one year he was not making a more just income he would quit and find a new position.

Diana was relieved by all the steps that George had taken, but George was not satisfied. He began to feel a moral obligation to confront his parents' drinking, especially that of his mother, who seemed to be in the late stages of alcoholism, with her health at risk. Over several sessions George planned and rehearsed how he would confront his mother.

During this time he also talked to his siblings about the family disease. They were initially defensive, and even though they gradually realized what was happening, they were unwilling to be part of a confrontation. At Sarah's advice George talked to an alcohol specialist, who worked with George and his siblings to set up a family intervention. After much practice and rehearsal, they confronted his mother about her drinking. Although no dramatic change occurred in his parents, George resolved that he would continue to bring up the issue and leave his parents' house whenever they began drinking.

But a striking change was occurring in George. He was becoming more confident and assertive. Diana was shocked at the way their marital interactions were changing now that George had begun to do some family-of-origin work.

Listening to George struggling with his family helped Diana understand her own family issues. Her father had deserted the family when she was two years old. Her mother's father had been an alcoholic and totally irresponsible. As a result her family was characterized by strong women and weak men. Diana realized that one of her strongly held beliefs was that men are irresponsible and not to be trusted; she remembered her mother saying repeatedly that men were lazy and irresponsible. Thus she unconsciously assumed that she would be the overresponsible one in the marriage. The more George withdrew, the more her beliefs about men were confirmed. Diana's family-of-origin work was to understand the role of women over the generations and the way they saw men as weak and ineffective. Diana needed to confront the reality that while she wanted George to take more responsibility and become more powerful, she had a hard time trusting him. She needed to struggle with letting go of powerful multigenerational messages, and not taking responsibility despite the multigenerational messages in her family about women needing to be strong and to take charge.

As both George and Diana struggled with powerful family-of-origin issues and with belief systems that distorted their communication, they began to feel much closer to each other. They were able to solve problems more effectively and experience more intimacy than they ever had. They acknowledged that they had a lot of issues still to work on with their respective families, but felt that they wanted to try that work on their own. Sarah agreed with them that they had made enormous strides, and suggested that they meet in a month to see how they were doing.

This case study displays the application of the integrative model to a mid-length case (35 sessions). Counseling involved problem solving, focusing on the communication style of the couple, examining the belief systems of both George and Diana, and finally exploring the family-of-origin issues of each. Diagram 6 summarizes the flow of treatment.

CASE STUDY 3: THE PACKERS

The Packers called Jon for a counseling appointment in early December. They explained that they wanted to work on both family and marital problems, and that they were in a state of crisis. They requested an appointment as soon as possible.

Gene was an engineer at a local corporation, with a great deal of responsibility, while Shirley was a supervising nurse in a hospital in a neighboring town. They had one son, Ray, who was sixteen; another son had died in an accident seven years ago at the age of six. Both of their parents were deceased. They reported all this information in a narrative tone in the first ten minutes of the session, as if they had told their story many times before. Indeed, Gene and Shirley were experienced clients, having seen three other marital therapists in the last six years. Because their minister had told them that Jon was one of the top marital therapists in the area, they expressed confidence that he could help them, although none of their previous therapists could.

Jon was already beginning to feel overwhelmed by this couple. He reviewed with them some of the work they had done in their previous therapies; it appeared that they had worked on problem-solving issues in an attempt to build better communication, and had even gone to several marriage enrichment weekends and several classes on couples communication. They had worked with another therapist on family-of-origin issues and had spent many hours researching their family histories and constructing elaborate genograms.

Despite all this effort and well-intentioned therapy, they seemed little better off than when they had started. They still tended to have fights that could rapidly escalate and turn physical. Their son Ray was out of control and beginning to flunk out of school. They were not able to help him; indeed

DIAGRAM 6
The Humfelts

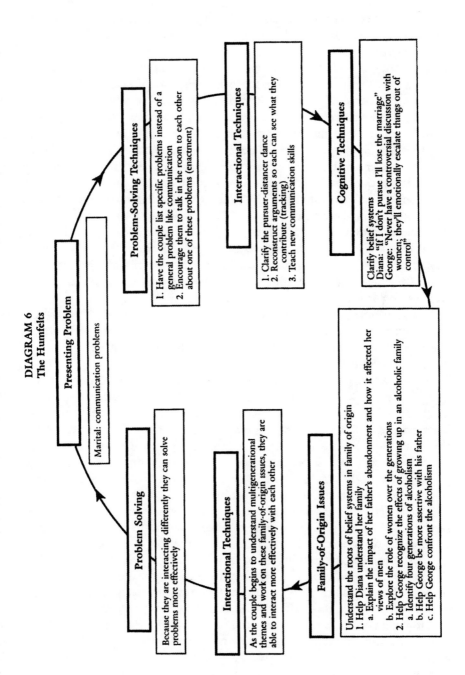

Presenting Problem

Marital: communication problems

Problem-Solving Techniques

1. Have the couple list specific problems instead of a general problem like communication
2. Encourage them to talk in the room to each other about one of these problems (enactment)

Interactional Techniques

1. Clarify the pursuer-distancer dance
2. Reconstruct arguments so each can see what they contribute (tracking)
3. Teach new communication skills

Cognitive Techniques

Clarify belief systems
Diana: "If I don't pursue I'll lose the marriage"
George: "Never have a controversial discussion with women; they'll emotionally escalate things out of control"

Problem Solving

Because they are interacting differently they can solve problems more effectively

Interactional Techniques

As the couple begins to understand multigenerational themes and work on these family-of-origin issues, they are able to interact more effectively with each other

Family-of-Origin Issues

Understand the roots of belief systems in family of origin
1. Help Diana understand her family
   a. Explain the impact of her father's abandonment and how it affected her views of men
   b. Explore the role of women over the generations
2. Help George recognize the effects of growing up in an alcoholic family
   a. Identify four generations of alcoholism
   b. Help George be more assertive with his father
   c. Help George confront the alcoholism

they contributed to his problem with their fighting. They informed Jon that if this therapy did not work, they would get a divorce—neither of them could take it anymore.

Jon's struggle was to know where to begin with this couple given all the material they were presenting. He chose to begin with problem-solving methodology, not because he had illusions that it would be effective, but because he thought it would reveal more accurately the interactional style of the couple.

As he encouraged the couple to talk in the session about what it would take to heal their marriage, their interaction heated up quickly. Shirley insisted that if only Gene would be more attentive to her and spend more time talking to her, their relationship would improve. Gene retorted that if Shirley would only back off and give him some space, he would be delighted to spend more time with her. He added sarcastically, "Who would want to spend time with her? She is so demanding and bossy. If I give her an inch, she will always take a mile." Shirley quickly responded, "All my friends at the hospital say I should have left him a long time ago. Maybe they are right." The argument strayed further from the original question and escalated rapidly until they were yelling at each other.

Jon interrupted before they got out of control and asked, "Is this how your arguments usually go?" Gene smiled and suggested that this was mild compared with many of the fights they had at home. "We have the scars to prove it," he added.

As one might predict, problem solving and working on communication with this couple was counterproductive. Although it was relatively simple to diagnose the pursuer-distancer dance of this couple and to help them understand their rapidly escalating interactions, it proved difficult to disrupt this cycle. Jon spent a number of sessions helping the couple track their interactions and think about alternate ways of responding to each other. In addition, he worked to help Shirley not pursue, and to help Gene attempt to take more initiative in the relationship.

They agreed to work on these changes between sessions, but the changes rarely held. The same themes emerged from session to session. Simply to continue to work on their dance would be an exercise in therapeutic futility. As a result Jon began exploring more explicitly their dominant belief systems.

This approach proved equally frustrating. As a bright and articulate couple who had been through years of couples therapy, they could quickly identify powerful beliefs that they held about each other. Shirley recognized her belief that if she did not pursue Gene he would probably withdraw into his hobbies more and more. She imagined that he would wind up playing golf and tennis all weekend, spending evenings working late in the office, and leaving no time for her. She could identify her fear that he would eventually become involved with another woman and then leave the marriage.

Gene could articulate his beliefs that Shirley wanted to control him and run every aspect of his life, even picking out the clothes he wore each day. He believed strongly that if he gave in on any points, Shirley would gain more and more control until he had no life whatsoever. As a result, Gene saw every issue as a battleground upon which he had to fight powerfully to keep Shirley from taking over.

The couple was initially excited to learn about each other's beliefs and even bought a popular book that applied the insights of cognitive psychology to marriage. For a few sessions the marriage seemed much better, and they assured Jon that he was by far the best marital therapist they had seen.

But their progress and enthusiasm tended to be short-lived. Although their relationship was slowly getting better, they had a long way to go—fights still tended to occur rapidly, with little provocation. After nearly twenty sessions spread over six months, Jon knew that this couple had much more work to do.

By May, the reality that their son might flunk his junior year and not graduate with his class the following year was beginning to hit them. The couple asked Jon to help them with their parenting style, and agreed to try to hold off on their own marital problems. Jon felt that this shift in focus might indirectly help the couple with their marriage, and at the same time help them with their parenting issues. By doing some structural work that aligns the couple to help one of their children, a counselor can often indirectly help a couple who are too conflicted maritally to respond to marital therapy. Some success in this parenting endeavor encourages the couple and they feel closer in their marriage.

But this strategy proved quite difficult with the Packers. As Jon reviewed with them their problem-solving approaches to Ray's school-related problems, they began to blame each other. Gene argued that because Shirley had always babied Ray and done all his homework for him, he had learned nothing about self-discipline and had never grown up. "You've ruined that boy because you could never set limits with him. You spoiled him rotten, and now look what we have." Shirley quickly retorted, "I had to give him extra to make up for all that you never provided. You gave far more to your business than to our son. Someone had to love him."

As he listened to the couple argue, Jon saw that from a structural perspective Shirley was enmeshed with Ray and quite overprotective, which was crippling his development. Jon could also see that Gene's lack of involvement with Ray contributed to the enmeshment between Shirley and Ray. Understanding the problem structurally, however, did not provide an easy solution. Jon attempted to coach Gene on some specific ways to be more involved with Ray, and tried to help Shirley back away from Ray more and help him face the consequences of his actions. But the couple came to have greater difficulty following through on what they agreed to during the sessions.

Having family sessions with Ray only intensified the problem. No matter what the couple was working on with their son, triangles quickly arose, with Ray aligning with one parent against the other. Jon continued to attempt to strengthen the fragile couple bond so that they could provide more effective parenting for their son. Somehow Ray passed all his courses by the end of June. This was a great boost to the couple, and for a while their relationship improved.

As the crisis passed, however, the couple drifted back to their former style of bickering and fighting; they seemed to need a crisis to keep them together. Jon reflected this perception to them. As they pondered it, they reviewed the many crises of their lives. Since childhood, both of them had had one crisis after another and one loss after another. Both Gene and Shirley had alcoholic parents who had not provided much for them. Both of them had become overresponsible in heroic attempts to compensate for their parents, thereby sacrificing their own childhood. Both had lost parents without being able to mourn their deaths or to resolve any resentments with their parents. Early in their marriage Shirley had had several surgeries that were life threatening. At that point Gene began to withdraw from her, perhaps unconsciously fearing that she might die. Their ultimate loss was the death of their second child in a tragic accident. Both prided themselves in getting on with life after his death and had determined not to talk much about it. From that point forward their marriage began to have serious problems.

They also had no extended family to support them: Gene was an only child, and they had lost contact with Shirley's only sister, who was in the late stages of alcoholism. This lack of support contributed to their problems. Their belief that the marriage could fill all the voids left by their cumulative losses set them up for more bitter disappointment.

As they looked at these losses, they realized that they had not only never mourned them but never even acknowledged their power. They had consistently minimized the traumas of their lives. These sessions were powerfully unsettling.

Jon knew that the only hope for this marriage was for the couple to mourn those losses and come to grips with the emptiness that both of them experienced on a continual basis. This process took months of painful work. Both Gene and Shirley were frightened—at times terrified—as they moved into their own emptiness. Sometimes they found it easier to turn sorrow and emptiness into anger, because the anger seemed easier to deal with. They would frequently move away from the subject of loss and mourning and resume fighting, coming back to the sessions with written notes on what the other had done wrong.

Rather than participate in this behavior, Jon pointed out to them that perhaps they needed to keep fighting because it gave them a common focus that kept them from the pain of facing their inner emptiness. Gene and Shirley looked puzzled for a moment and said they did not understand. Gene added, "Why in the world would we keep fighting? That's what we are spending thousands of dollars on therapy over the last six years to try and stop." Jon gently responded, "The two of you have had more losses and tragedy in your lives than anyone I know. You have lost your parents, a child, and even your own childhoods because of the alcoholism in your families. Fighting at least blocks the pain for a while and provides a common focus." The couple seemed to understand.

Over the next six months therapy continued to focus on their emptiness and loss. As part of examining their losses, they looked in detail at the role of alcoholism in each of their families and its effect on them as children. At Jon's suggestion they began attending adult children of alcoholics (ACoA) groups, partly to help them realize that their reactions to their experiences were normal, and partly because they desperately needed support.

Many of their sessions were more like individual therapy with one while the other observed. This approach accomplished several purposes: first, it slowed down their reactivity; second, it allowed them to get more in touch with the power of their individual losses and issues; finally, it allowed Jon to model empathy for them.

As they continued to work on family-of-origin issues and on individual issues, they gradually changed. Their fights became less intense and less frequent, and they were occasionally able to stop arguments from going out of control. They were also able eventually to work together to set boundaries for their son. Jon helped them see that in so doing they were opening up new possibilities for the future.

In view of all that this couple had experienced during their lives, therapy could not be short nor would the changes be dramatic. Their therapy lasted nearly three years, going back and forth between interactional issues, parenting issues, examining belief systems, exploring family-of-origin material, and looking at individual issues. For the last six months of treatment, they met with Jon once a month to test how much they had internalized the changes. Three months later a follow-up session revealed that although they were not an ideal couple, they were doing well and were continuing to attend an adult children of alcoholics group in their community. Diagram 7 summarizes their treatment.

CONCLUSION

In examining these three case studies it should be apparent that the integrative model can be applied to a variety of types of couples and families. It has both long- and short-term application and can be customized to each family's particular needs. The model provides a way of integrating theory and of building assessment and treatment maps, which ought to keep treatment moving in a clear direction.

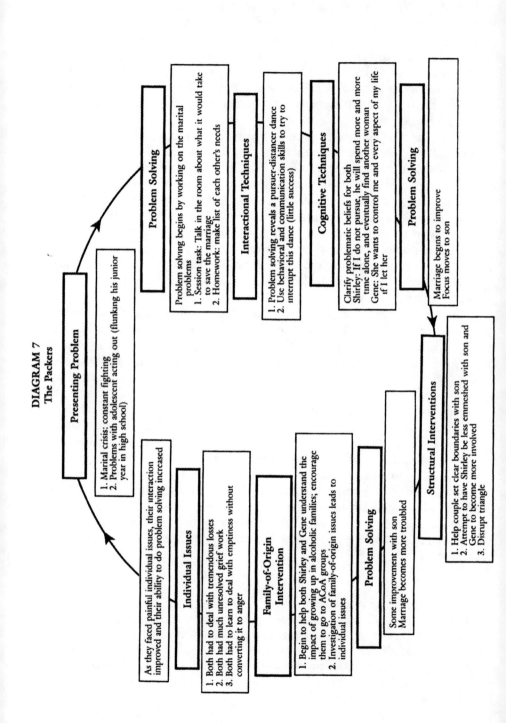

DIAGRAM 7
The Packers

Presenting Problem
1. Marital crisis; constant fighting
2. Problems with adolescent acting out (flunking his junior year in high school)

Problem Solving
Problem solving begins by working on the marital problems
1. Session task: Talk in the room about what it would take to save the marriage
2. Homework: make list of each other's needs

Interactional Techniques
1. Problem solving reveals a pursuer-distancer dance
2. Use behavioral and communication skills to try to interrupt this dance (little success)

Cognitive Techniques
Clarify problematic beliefs for both
Shirley: If I do not pursue, he will spend more and more time alone, and eventually find another woman
Gene: She wants to control me and every aspect of my life if I let her

Problem Solving
Marriage begins to improve
Focus moves to son

As they faced painful individual issues, their interaction improved and their ability to do problem solving increased

Individual Issues
1. Both had to deal with tremendous losses
2. Both had much unresolved grief work
3. Both had to learn to deal with emptiness without converting it to anger

Family-of-Origin Intervention
1. Begin to help both Shirley and Gene understand the impact of growing up in alcoholic families; encourage them to go to ACoA groups
2. Investigation of family-of-origin issues leads to individual issues

Problem Solving
Some improvement with son
Marriage becomes more troubled

Structural Interventions
1. Help couple set clear boundaries with son
2. Attempt to have Shirley be less enmeshed with son and Gene to become more involved
3. Disrupt triangle

BIBLIOGRAPHY

Bateson, G.
    1972   *Steps to an Ecology of Mind.* New York: Jason Aronson.

Beavers, W. R.
    1977   *Psychotherapy and Growth: A Family Systems Perspective.* New York: Brunner/Mazel.

Beck, A.
    1976   *Cognitive Therapy and Emotional Disorders.* New York: International Universities Press.
    1988   *Love Is Never Enough.* New York: Harper and Row.

Bowen, M.
    1978   *Family Therapy in Clinical Practice.* New York: Jason Aronson.

Brown, F.
    1991   *Reweaving the Family Tapestry.* New York: W. W. Norton.

Carter, E., and M. McGoldrick, eds.
    1980   *The Family Life Cycle: A Framework for Family Therapy.* New York: Gardner Press.

Ellis, A.
    1977   "The Basic Clinical Theory of Rational-Emotive Therapy" in Ellis, A., and Grieger, R., eds., *Handbook of Rational Emotive Therapy.* Volume 1. New York: Springer.

Framo, J.
    1992   *Family of Origin Therapy.* New York: Brunner/Mazel Publishers.

Friedman, E.
    1985   *Generation to Generation: Family Process in Church and Synagogue.* New York: Guilford Press.

Haley, J.
    1976   *Problem Solving Therapy.* San Francisco: Jossey-Bass.

Hendrix, H.
    1988   *Getting the Love You Want.* New York: Henry Holt and Company.

Mahler, M., F. Pine, and A. Bergman.
    1975   *The Psychological Birth of the Human Infant: Symbiosis and Individuation.* New York: Basic Books.

McGoldrick, M., and R. Gersen.
    1985   *Genograms in Family Assessment.* New York: W. W. Norton.

Minuchin, S.
    1974   *Families and Family Therapy.* Cambridge, Mass.: Harvard University Press.

Minuchin, S., and C. Fishman.
    1981   *Family Therapy Techniques.* Cambridge, Mass.: Harvard University Press.
Offer, D., and M. Sabshin.
    1974   *Normality: Theoretical and Clinical Aspects of Mental Health.* Rev. ed.
            New York: Basic Books.
Olson, D., C. Russell, and D. Sprenkle, eds.
    1989   *Circumplex Model: Systemic Assessment and Treatment of Families.* New
            York: Haworth Press.
Palazzoli, M., et al.
    1978   *Paradox and Counterparadox.* New York: Jason Aronson.
Reid, W.
    1985   *Family Problem Solving.* New York: Columbia University Press.
Roberto, L.
    1992   *Transgenerational Family Therapies.* New York: Guilford Press.
Sager, C.
    1976   *Marriage Contracts and Couples Therapy.* New York: Brunner/Mazel.
Scharff, D., and J. Scharff.
    1987   *Object Relations Family Therapy.* New York: Jason Aronson.
    1991   *Object Relations Couple Therapy.* New York: Jason Aronson.
Scharff, J., editor.
    1989   *Foundations of Object Relations Family Therapy.* New York: Jason Aron-
            son.
Shapiro, R., and J. Zinner.
    1989   "Family Organization and Adolescent Development." In Scharff and
            Scharff 1987, 81.
Slipp, S.
    1984   *Object Relations: A Dynamic Bridge Between Individual and Family Treat-
            ment.* New York: Jason Aronson.
    1988   *The Technique and Practice of Object Relations Family Therapy.* New York:
            Jason Aronson.
Walsh, F., editor.
    1982   *Normal Family Processes.* New York: Guilford Press.
Watzlawick, P., J. Beavin, and D. Jackson.
    1967   *Pragmatics of Human Communication: A Study of Interactional Patterns,
            Pathologies, and Paradoxes.* New York: W. W. Norton.

Printed in the United States
125755LV00001B/58-63/A